Curse of the Silver Screen

Tragedy & Disaster Behind the Movies

By John W. Law

aplomb publishing
San Francisco

Curse of the Silver Screen by John W. Law
Published by Aplomb Publishing, San Francisco, California. 1999
Copyright 1998.

Library of Congress Catalog Card Number:
98-73380

ISBN 09665676-0-9

1st edition

Manufactured in the United States of America.

No part of this publication may be reproduced or transmitted in any form or by any means, electronic or mechanical including photocopying, recording, or by any information storage or retrieval system, without written permission from the publisher. Photographs reprinted with permission where required. Any questions regarding copyright permission should be directed to the publisher in writing, Aplomb Publishing, P.O. Box 210126, San Francisco, California 94121.

Dedicated to those who love not only what goes on the silver screen, but what goes on behind it.

Acknowledgements

It would be impossible to acknowledge all those who assisted, knowingly and unknowingly, in the production of this book. The back of this book lists a number of sources used in the research that led to what you see before you. The author gratefully thanks these resources, for the book would have not been possible without them. In addition, the author wishes to thank any and all who provided interviews, offered comments, suggestions and insight that made the book come together. Special thanks goes out to my family, as well as Tom Moulton, Suzanne Stack, Elizabeth Carmen and Don Ferguson for their support and assistance. Thanks to Marcela Barrientos, Steve Johnson and Kris Matsuyama for design assistance and Stu Selland for photography. In addition, thanks to the Cinema Shop in San Francisco and Memorabilia Mine in San Jose for help gathering the photographs that complement the stories chronicled here. Finally, thanks to those whose influence, style and journalistic integrity helped shape this author, especially the journalists from my years with Suburban Publications, the Alameda Newspaper Group and The Observer. In particular, Marianne Schmitt, Helen Cooper, Catherine Puleo, David Hickey, Lydia Forte Roberts, Lyndon Hickerson, Dave Burket, Dennis Daylor, Chris Campos, Phyllis Sherman, Jean Patterson and Andrea Gregg.

Table of Contents

- Introduction — 1
- Did Satan Curse *Rosemary's Baby*? — 5
- Fate Catches Up with *The Misfits* — 19
- Obsession Casts a Shadow Over *Marnie* — 29
- A Costly *Cleopatra* — 41
- Doomed Rebels — 51
- Tragedy Hits *Raintree County* — 63
- Tragedy Stalks the Stars of *The Conqueror* — 73
- Crawford Cursed by *Trog* — 85
- Terror of *The Exorcist* - On and Off Screen — 97
- Stars of *Superman* Suffer Tragedy — 111
- Conclusion — 125
- Bibliography — 127
- Index — 139

Introduction

Success is measured in a variety of ways. Whether it be monetary value, stature, look, feel and time, objects can only be as successful as a consumer allows them to be. Film embodies this subjective reality.

In the arena of film, success is often measured on a scale of dollars. Cost of a film is balanced with the box office receipts it draws. But in addition to dollars, critical acclaim, celebrity, special effects and direction, a host of other factors are used to measure success in the film industry. Time also plays a major factor. How we as viewers see a film 10, 20 or 50 years later can play a part in success as well. A poorly reviewed film can return as a classic feature years later and spawn books, sequels and legendary tales. Alfred Hitchcock's *Psycho* suffered mediocre to poor reviews initially, but patrons lined up to see the film and by the year's end in 1960, many of those reviewers had reevaluated the film as one of the best of the year. And now, more than 35 years later the film is regarded as one of the greatest movies of all time.

Tragedy and Disaster Behind the Movies

The conditions under which a film was made play a crucial factor in the final film and possibly on its evaluation by critics and moviegoers. *Waterworld*, the 1995 futuristic epic starring Kevin Costner, received so much publicity prior to release about its reported $180 million price tag that it was almost doomed to fail. Critics and fans were virtually unable to disregard the publicity and evaluate the film simply for the movie itself. The enormous cost magnified expectations to a point that the film could not live up to. Critics and moviegoers alike regarded the film as a flop even though its worldwide box office receipts and subsequent video rentals drew back most of the money.

The personal lives of the stars involved, exotic location shoots and the times in which movies are made also play a role in the final product. Romances on the set, accidents and even noteworthy news events play a part in how a film gets made. Sometimes the films themselves are noteworthy news.

Included in this book are a number of films that are noteworthy. Not because they are classic motion pictures, although some are. Not because they were very costly or box office bombs, although some were. The history of these films is fascinating because of events surrounding their making. What happened during the filming of these motion pictures affected the lives of those who played a part and sometimes even those who did not. Fate played a part in each of these films. Strange events, eerie happenings or just uncanny bad luck caused each of these films to be remembered, often more because of those events than for the work captured by the camera.

Whether it's three young stars together onscreen in *Rebel Without a Cause,* who each suffered violent deaths while still quite young, or a cast and crew who filmed a forgettable film on radioactive land not far from nuclear testing in *The Conqueror*, these films each have a story to tell.

An aging star whose career came to an abrupt close after making a box office bomb, or the events surrounding what some call the costliest movie ever made, the story these films have to tell was not written in the script. Yet, it's often much more fascinating, and many cases, much more tragic.

The horrifying news of Charles Manson's rampage and its

bizarre tie to the smash hit *Rosemary's Baby,* or the death of an actor in *The Exorcist* shortly after his character's death in the movie make these films fascinating to watch, taking into account the events surrounding their making and release.

Stars like Marilyn Monroe and Clark Gable faced off for the first time together onscreen in *The Misfits*, a film that would make the final screen appearance for each. Or the friendship of Montgomery Clift and Elizabeth Taylor, and how that friendship caused tragic results during the making of *Raintree County,* are stories that have long outlasted the movies themselves. Even the trouble-filled production of *Superman* and its impact on exploding budgets and huge celebrity salaries lives on when its stars suffer a series of personal tragedies.

The public's enduring fascination with celebrities and cultural icons has spawned generations of moviegoers. With the industry of filmmaking more than a century old, society and movie-making are intertwined. Films are ripped from today's headlines and today's headlines are even drawn from film. Oliver Stone's features *JFK* and *Nixon* capture historic events of the 20th century, even though critics debate how much of the "fact" is fiction. And in the reverse, movies impact real life when events on the big screen make it into everyday life. A scene from the film *Money Train* gripped headlines when youths set a subway token booth on fire with a New York City public transportation worker inside.

The films chronicled in the coming chapters each tell a different story. Whether truly cursed or simply fascinating additions to the films themselves, these stories are merely one more layer to the rich and expansive history of filmmaking.

Tragedy and Disaster Behind the Movies

Rosemary's Baby

1968

Tragedy and Disaster Behind the Movies

Did Satan Curse *Rosemary's Baby?*

Producer William Castle claimed a curse on the film nearly killed him and took the lives of several others

❝ Bastard. Believer of Witchcraft. Worshiper at the Shrine of Satanism. My prediction is you will slowly rot during a long and painful illness which you have brought upon yourself."

The words were written by a moviegoer in 1968. The "bastard" was William Castle, producer of the film *Rosemary's Baby,* a film about the birth of Satan's child.

The film, based on a 1967 book of the same name by Ira Levin, was a blockbuster. It earned some $30 million at the box office, captured one Academy Award and was nominated for another, earned a Golden Globe Award and a Photoplay Award, and garnered Castle a nomination for Producer of the Year from the

Producers Guild.

And although the film earned Castle his first major critically-acclaimed success and put him on the verge of brilliant career as producer of mainstream "A" pictures, the film also set forth what Castle believed was a curse that nearly cost him his life and took the lives of several others.

The Making of a Horror King

William Castle's claim to fame came in the 1950s as the director and producer of "B" horror flicks that were marketed with gimmicks and off-the-wall promotions. His career in show business started in 1929 when, at the age of 15, he had the opportunity to be Bela Lugosi's assistant stage manager in the stage production of *Dracula*. It was here that Castle got his first taste of behind-the-scenes horror and the promotion of it.

After years of directing, producing and acting in lesser-known plays and movies, Castle found his niche creating campy horror. Films like *The Tingler, 13 Ghosts, House on Haunted Hill, Strait-Jacket*, and *I Saw What You Did* used gimmicks like life insurance policies against death by fright, electrically-charged seats to scare moviegoers, and "Fright-Breaks" to rake in box office receipts from teenagers looking for a good scare. But many of his films were panned by critics and have gone down in film history as schlock horror.

Producer William Castle

In 1967, Castle received galley proofs of *Rosemary's Baby* from literary agent Marvin Birdt, and according to his 1976 autobiography, Castle had no intention of even reading the book, let alone making the movie. "You know the bottom has fallen out of horror films," Castle told Birdt.

"They'll knock you on your ass," replied Birdt of the

proofs. Castle agreed to read the proofs at home that evening and finished them in three hours knowing he had to make the movie.

A Movie is Born

The asking price to purchase the rights to the book was a quarter of a million dollars and Castle didn't have that sort of money. He wanted to think about it, but was told he'd better act fast because someone else was interested in it. The other person was rumored to be Alfred Hitchcock.

Now, Castle had been watching Hitchcock for years. To create first-rate thrillers and horrors was his dream and Hitchcock was the master. Drawing big-name talent to his films, like Hitchcock did, was another one of his goals. In the 60s, Castle succeeded in getting Joan Crawford and Barbara Stanwyck to star in his films and he'd worked with Vincent Price on several occasions, but his films never came close to Hitchcock's with the critics. In 1961, he even made his own *Psycho,* called *Homicidal,* in which a knife-weilding woman, dressed as a man, goes "psycho." But the film never quite lived up to a Hitchcock thriller. Castle knew *Rosemary's Baby* was his chance to shine.

Hitchcock supposedly turned down the film rights, but Castle on the other hand offered $100,000 in cash and five percent of 100 percent of the profits. And if the book became a best seller, Castle promised an additional $50,000. Twenty-four hours later his deal was accepted.

Castle had planned to direct the movie, but Paramount Studios, who negotiated to film the horror, had another idea. They offered him $250,000 and 50 percent of the profits to produce the film. But for direction, Paramount had someone else in mind.

"Have you ever heard of Roman Polanski?" asked Charles Bluhdorn, one of the head executives at Paramount.

"Of course," answered Castle who knew of Polanski's flair for filmmaking and his early classic *Knife in the Water.*

"If Polanski, with his youth, directed *Rosemary's Baby,* and you, with your experience, produced. You could teach each other so much," said Bluhdorn.

"No deal," said Castle.

But in time, Castle agreed to meet Polanski and found his ideas about the film suitable to his own. Castle bowed to Paramount and Polanski would direct the film. Polanski then adapted the screenplay and set forth to film the movie. His salary was only $150,000 with no net of the proceeds.

When it came to casting the role of Rosemary, Castle won out. Polanski wanted Tuesday Weld for the lead role, while Castle saw Mia Farrow. Robert Redford was chosen for the role of Rosemary's husband, but because of legal troubles with Paramount he was dropped from consideration. Jack Nicholson was reportedly interested in the role, but John Cassavetes eventually was chosen for the part. And for the neighbors, Minnie and Roman Castevet, Ruth Gordan and Sidney Blackmer were chosen. Once the rest of the casting was rounded out production began.

Filming of a Horror Classic

Troubles on the set began almost immediately after production began in the fall of 1967, according to Castle. Polanski was known as a perfectionist, claimed Castle, and in the first six hours of shooting not a single shot was captured. "I was amazed at Roman's eye for detail," said Castle in his autobiography. "A perfectionist, he refused to compromise. If I had been directing the picture, I could have finished the scene in several hours. Polanski was taking several nights."

In another slow process, Polanski set the story in 1965 and insisted that every furnishing and item of clothing match the year. And while it was only two years earlier, the process became cumbersome.

The crew fell days behind schedule and Castle feared Paramount might shut down production. He urged Polanski to speed up the process, but Polanski refused to bend. "*Rosemary* will be a blockbuster, but I will not compromise. You understand, don't you?" said Polanski.

The first fatality of the production came in the form of a marriage. Mia Farrow had recently married Frank Sinatra and Sinatra had planned to star with his wife in his next film. But because *Rosemary's Baby* was behind schedule, Farrow would never be finished before the next production began.

"Mia's supposed to start my picture on Monday. Will she be finished by then?" asked Sinatra on the phone to Castle, who was amazed to be talking to Sinatra, but knew he didn't have an answer that would please him.

"No, Frank, I'm afraid that's impossible. Even by working Saturdays, she'll be at least three weeks," replied Castle.

"Then I'm pulling her off your picture tomorrow," said Sinatra.

"That'll mean shutting us down, Frank."

"Sorry to do that to you, Bill, but there's no other choice."

But there was another choice. And it was Mia Farrow's. She decided she wanted to finish the picture and her marriage felt the blow. Rumors said Sinatra threatened to divorce her if she didn't walk off the picture. And when she didn't, the story goes that Sinatra sent his lawyers to Polanski's offices during filming to deliver her the divorce papers. The marriage didn't last the year.

Another problem on the set was a clash of personalities between Polanski and Cassavetes. Shouting matches between the director and his leading male star were said to be commonplace during filming and their dislike for each other only grew as production dragged on. And the fact that Cassavetes was a director made the conflict worse as each insulted the other's style and work.

Eventually the production did come to an end and the film was cut and everyone was sure they had a winner on their hands. And they were right.

A Box Office Success

The film proved to be the success Paramount was looking for after its release in June 1968. Total cost of the production was reported at a mere $2.3 million. The film, in its original release took in more than $15 million in box-office receipts, becoming the 34th largest money-making film of the decade and one of Paramount's top five money-makers of the 60s, eventually grossing more than $30 million.

Critics were mixed about the film. Some felt Polanski pulled off a fantastic effort, while others were left less ecstatic. Reviewer for *The New York Times*, Vincent Canby wrote, "Mia Farrow is quite marvelous, pale, suffering, almost constantly on screen in a difficult role that requires her to be learning for almost two hours what the audience has guessed from the start. ... for most of its length the film has nothing to be excited about ... nothing cumulative — to fill that time with suspense. But the good side of that is that you can see the movie, and like it, without risking terrors or nightmares."

As the box office receipts flowed in, so did the mail. Castle claimed in his autobiography that he received an average of 50 hate letters a day after the film's initial release. "I've received crank letters on my other pictures," he wrote. "but none like these."

The letters called him a Satan worshiper, a purveyor of evil and said his soul would "forever burn in hell."

He tossed them off knowing it was one of the costs of success and looked to his bright future knowing the hit picture would be leading to profits and an opportunity to have his pick of projects. But, in addition to the nasty letters, a number of religious groups publicly blasted the film urging the public to boycott the film. But the publicity only added to the appeal, drawing moviegoers to the theater to see what all the commotion was about.

Director Roman Polanski

Castle's next offer came in the form of a dark comedy. Neil Simon's *The Out of Towners* offered Castle a chance to move on. It would be a major departure for Castle and another mainstream, critical success could put him on the map of major motion pictures. The producer's job was offered to him and he wanted it. No sooner had he agreed to go to New York and settle the deal than he felt a pain in his groin.

A Curse Takes Hold

He thought it was just indigestion and he'd be in New York by Monday, but it was not to be. The pain grew worse, nausea followed and the room began to spin. He blacked out. It was Halloween and they found him unconscious on the floor of his home when his wife and children returned from trick-or-treating.

At the hospital they found there was a blockage. He drank lots of fluids, but could not urinate. He couldn't feel his legs. In surgery they gave him a spinal and finally the blockage began to come free. After six days he was able to go home.

Then it happened again. Back in the hospital and more surgery. It was kidney stones the size of small rocks. He was home again in two weeks.

Then it happened again.

Then again.

More time in the hospital and more surgery. He began to believe the letters of hate and the curse of *Rosemary's Baby.* He feared it was going to kill him he said. "The story of *Rosemary's Baby* was happening in life. Witches, all of them, were casting their spell, and I was becoming one of the principal players."

While Castle was battling his own evils in the hospital, fate struck again.

Christopher Komeda, the composer of *Rosemary's Baby*, had a blood clot suddenly rupture in his brain while skiing. He was admitted to the same hospital as Castle. He was in a coma. A short time later, after he had been awarded a Golden Globe award as composer for the film, Komeda died.

Castle no longer could stand on his own. He began seeing the best urologists he could find searching for a cure. There was a stone causing the main obstruction. Castle could no longer handle the surgery and feared he was going to die.

The only alternative was sodium bicarbonate injections. They were painful, but they might dissolve the stone. Castle decided it was better than surgery and took the injections. They were given twice a day, every day and caused him to suffer high fevers. Weeks turned into months and it looked like surgery would have to follow. But finally the stone began to dissolve. Castle began to get well. He thought the curse had lifted.

Tragedy Continues

Back when Roman Polanski agreed to direct *Rosemary's Baby* he needed a place to live in California after the filming was finished in New York and at least for the duration the the picture. Castle claims he agreed to help him find a home before filming began. Polanski wanted a place near the ocean. Polanski's fiance, Sharon Tate, would be the one to decide on the place.

Castle found a home in Malibu, but later, deciding they wanted a larger home, Polanski and Tate moved to a place hidden at the end of a lonely winding road on Bel Air hill in Benedict Canyon. The redwood house was at 10050 Cielo Drive and had a large lawn, a swimming pool and a guest house. The owner was a Hollywood business manager who had leased the home to the son of Doris Day, Terry Melcher, who was living there with his girlfriend, actress/model Candice Bergen. Melcher was moving and decided to sublet the house. Tate loved the place.

But Tate was not aware of Melcher's tie to a bizarre character named Charles Manson. It appears that Melcher, who was best known as a Hollywood record producer, was being pestered by Manson for a record contract. Manson, who lived with Beach Boy Dennis Wilson for a time and developed some of his music contacts through him, considered himself a would-be musician and sent Melcher some recordings he had made. Melcher never took any interest in the tapes and ignored him. But Manson became bitter, even showing up at his home looking for the demo tapes he had sent.

When Manson arrived at 10050 Cielo Drive Tate's personal photographer Shahrokh Haiami answered the door but didn't recognize the name Melcher and turned Manson away. Tate appeared at the door as he was leaving and reportedly asked "Who was that guy?" Manson supposedly turned back and looked at Tate, then left the scene. He had no idea Melcher had moved.

Later that night Manson reportedly told his followers, "You're going out on Devil's business tonight," and sent them to 10050 Cielo Drive, telling them "No one must survive." Some stories suggest vengeance against Melcher led to the crime.

Four of Manson's "disciples," Tex Watson, Susan Atkins, Patricia Krenwikle and Linda Kasabian, arrived at the house, Saturday night, August 9, 1969. Steve Parent an 18-year-old friend of caretaker, William Garretson, was leaving guest house about 12:18 am when the killers arrived. He was shot and killed in his car, but no one heard the killing. Watson, Atkins and Krenwikle then entered the main house, with Kasabian keeping lookout outside. They confronted Voytek Frykowski, a friend of Polanski's who was staying at the house with his girlfriend, Abigail Folger, heir to the Folger coffee fortune. In addition to Frykowski and Folger, Jay Sebring, Hollywood hairdresser and one-time boyfriend to Sharon Tate, was spending the night to keep Tate company while Polanski was in Europe on movie business. The four were herded into the living room and then stabbed and beaten to death.

The word "PIG" was scrawled on the white floor of the living room in Tate's blood. Manson was not present at the killings, but was later convicted of the murders along with the others.

Actress Mia Farrow was praised for her starring role in 'Rosemary's Baby.'

Manson and his followers continued their murder spree by killing Leno and Rosemary LaBianca in Los Feliz in another grizzly murder scene and ranch hand Donald Shea was also killed, but his body was not found until eight years later. Gary Hinman, a friend of the Manson tribe was also killed at his Topanga home weeks before the killing spree by another of Manson's followers.

The murders looked like a ritualistic killing but at first the Tate and LaBianca killings were not linked. Polanski was questioned by the police and for a time was a suspect in the killings. There were stories of drugs and black magic and the Satanic story behind *Rosemary's Baby* fueled rumors for months about the killings.

Castle saw the headlines while he was just beginning to recuperate from his own brush with death and saw it as another part of the curse. And as the acclaim of his latest film came he no longer cared. Castle wrote: "Ironically, all my life I had yearned for the applause, approval and recognition from my peers; and when the awards were being passed out, I no longer cared. I was at home, very frightened of *Rosemary's Baby,* and still very ill.

The murders had all of Hollywood cloaked in fear. Frank Sinatra was said to be in hiding and Mia Farrow refused to attend Tate's funeral because it was reported she was afraid she would be next. Many stars beefed up security and began carrying guns and there were numerous offers of rewards for catching the killers.

Castle himself physically recovered from *Rosemary's Baby*, but his career never did. Although he did continue to work for nearly a decade after the film, none of his films equaled the success of *Rosemary's Baby.* And while the *Out of Towners* might have given Castle new-found success and the acclaim he desired, what he called the curse of *Rosemary's Baby* cost him that as well. The film was made without him.

On May 31, 1977, William Castle died of a heart attack. He believed, until the day he died, that there was a curse on *Rosemary's Baby.* Roman Polanski, on the other hand, has never supported that belief.

Curse of the Silver Screen

But the tale of a curse doesn't end there. The film has several other bizarre coincidences. In the film a character named Theresa commits suicide after learning that the Castavets are conspiring to have her impregnated by the devil. She jumps to her death landing in the same spot where John Lennon was shot to death by Mark David Chapman in 1980. Chapman, some say, met a man named Kenneth Anger in the late 1970s in Hawaii where Chapman gave Anger two silver bullets for luck. Anger was a small time director, who in the 60s made a film called *Lucifer Rising*. The film starred Bobby Beausoleil, a friend of Anger's. Beausoleil was the one who, reportedly on orders of Charles Manson, murdered Gary Hinman.

Beausoleil was caught by police shortly after the killing, but Manson supposedly plotted to get him out by staging copycat killings to lead police to believe Hinman's real killer was still on the loose. The Manson family killings of Sharon Tate and friends and the LaBianca couple may have been carried out only to free Beausoleil. And the ironic ties between the movie and the murders may have simply been coincidence after all.

Tragedy and Disaster Behind the Movies

Curse of the Silver Screen

The Misfits

1961

Tragedy and Disaster Behind the Movies

Fate catches up with *The Misfits*

Marilyn Monroe, Clark Gable give their final performances in a troubled classic motion picture

S tar power often plays a key role in the success of a film. The right name can sell big box office to even the worst of movies, but sometimes, which is the case with several films detailed in this book, star names aren't enough to salvage a movie. Sometimes, the forces are just against a film from the getgo. Such is the case with *The Misfits*.

In many ways, the film seemed destined for success. A successful story adapted for the big screen by the talented writer who gave the story life. It was even specifically written for the star actress who played the leading lady. In addition, an Oscar-winning director and a cast of stars that created numerous hit films, like *Gone With The Wind, From Here To Eternity, Rear Window* and *The Seven Year Itch,* spelled box office hit.

It was in the mid-1950s when Arthur Miller came across the idea for the story. Miller was living in a cabin in Nevada where he had come to establish residency to obtain a divorce from his current wife. It was there he met three cowboys who made their living by hunting wild horses.

The story fascinated Miller and he wanted to put it into words. But because the story didn't seem to fit his usual format — a play — he decided to craft it into a short story which he sold to *Esquire* magazine.

Miller became secretly involved with Marilyn Monroe in 1955 after her marriage to Joe DiMaggio ended. The lovers married on July 1, 1956 and sometime later Miller decided to transform the short story into a screenplay for his new bride.

Clark Gable and Marylin Monroe in 'The Misfits.'

And with the story created as a vehicle starring Monroe, the screenplay found its way into production, but the process took several years, as it usually does in Hollywood. And as the years wore on, the marriage between Miller and Monroe began to crumble. Monroe suffered three miscarriages, and each loss, coupled with her well-publicized neuroses, put a definite strain on the marriage. By the time the picture was ready for filming the marriage was coming to an end.

Around 1959, Monroe had been involved with co-star Yves Montand during *Let's Make Love*, but by the end of filming the affair had fizzled and Monroe was crushed. It is hard to imagine that Miller was unaware of the affair and that too may have made the situation shaky. Delays in finishing that production led to delays in starting *The Misfits*.

The Filming

In July 1960, *The Misfits* was finally set to begin shooting. In addition to Monroe and Miller, the key players included director John Huston and stars Clark Gable, Montgomery Clift, Thelma Ritter and Eli Wallach.

Filming took place in the Nevada desert during a summer of sweltering heat. Temperatures cracking the 100-degree mark made filming almost unbearable as cast and crew struggled to get through each day in their desert surroundings. Monroe herself was called "radiant" as filming began, but in a short time her absences became all too noticeable and tempers flared.

Monroe's unhappiness had her turning to drugs and alcohol to get through the filming, but the heat, tied with the Nembutal and the vodka and champagne made her useless and filming was often held up while cast and crew waited to see if she'd show up on the set. Gable, who was 59 years old, did most of his own stunts during the filming because he was bored waiting around for his other actors to show up, unaware what the intense heat and strenuous activity could be doing to his health.

Miller had his own troubles with the script, which needed major rewriting, and distanced himself from his wife in order to get his work done. This only made things worse, and reportedly led to

Monroe spreading rumors that Miller was involved in an affair with Huston's script assistant.

Even so, Monroe was excited to be working with Gable, who was at the end of his career. She had looked to him as a father figure and in younger years, stories say, she even told people he was her father.

As for Gable, he recognized her talent as an actress, but her problems on the set caused him great discomfort. When filming ended, Gable commented "What the hell is that girl's problem? Goddamn it, I like her, but she's so damn unprofessional. I damn near went nuts up there in Reno waiting for her to show. Christ, she didn't show up until after lunch some days, and then she would blow take after take ... I know she's heavy into booze and pills. Huston told me that. I think there's something wrong with the marriage. Too bad. I like Arthur, but that marriage ain't long for this world. Christ, I'm glad this picture's finished. She damn near gave me a heart attack."

Monroe wasn't the only one with emotional troubles. Montgomery Clift had struggled for years with the difficulty of being a movie star. And while *The Misfits* filming went surprisingly well for Clift, it was not without some turmoil. In addition to the heat and the trouble with Monroe, Clift had to overcome the fears of dealing with the cast of talent he was working with. In addition to Huston's well-known talent for directing, Clift was in awe of the ability of his co-stars.

Clift suffered severe anxiety over performing with his co-stars. In one scene, the script had Clift in a telephone booth while the remaining cast, including Monroe, Gable, Eli Wallach and well-known character actress Thelma Ritter, was sitting in a car listening to him speak to his mother on the pay phone. Clift recalled the scene as "frightening" and described it as an "audition" in front of "the gods and goddesses of the performing arts." Clift got the scene on the first take and quickly won over cast and crew.

A major credit for the success of Clift on the picture came from that fact that his role was not a difficult one. He was only featured in a few key scenes and Clift himself admitted that this was one of the reasons he decided to do the film. In an interview

Clift said "I decided to do *The Misfits* because I don't appear on the screen until page 57. In my last two pictures I was on the screen constantly."

Clift biographers added that had the star been in nearly every scene, like Monroe or Gable, his endurance would never have held out for the entire production. Huston once said that he found Clift to be a wonderful actor, but said he was "pretty much shredded" by the time he began to work with him.

Drugs on the Set

Although Clift performed well throughout much of the production, his addiction to drugs was also a well-known secret in Hollywood, but compared to Monroe he managed to control it much better while working. Clift also had a more varied drug addiction and used the drugs for different effects. In addition, Monroe and Clift used drugs for different reasons. Clift's had more to do with his personal demons, while Monroe's sprang from her intense insecurity and professional self-doubt.

Monroe's insecurities have been well-chronicled. In regards to *The Misfits*, her fear was nearly overwhelming. This was the first dramatic role she had faced in 11 years and Monroe was portraying what may have been the toughest role of her career — herself. Arthur Miller had written the role particularly for her, even using lines she had spoken to him in real life. This supposedly gave her incredible stage fright that nearly engulfed her and made performing nearly impossible.

The effect of the drugs was tremendous. When production began, filming started as early as 10 a.m., but soon the drugs kept Monroe from starting until 1 p.m. and then sometimes it wasn't until 4 p.m. that she began actually working. Director John Huston recalled that Monroe "would come to the set and she'd be in her dressing room, and sometimes we'd wait the whole morning. Occasionally she'd be practically *non compos mentis*. I remember saying to Miller, 'If she goes on at the rate she's going she'll be in an institution in two or three years, or dead.' It was in the way of being an indictment against Miller, and then I discovered he had no power whatever over her."

If those problems weren't bad enough, things grew worse when forest fires ravaged the Sierras and massive clouds of black smoke filled the skies. The clouds were so thick that they blocked the sunlight and prevented filming. The electric power also failed and filming again came to a halt.

No sooner had that situation cleared up when another problem hit. On August 27, 1960 Monroe overdosed and had to have her stomach pumped. She was flown to Los Angeles where she spent the next 10 days in Westside Hospital recovering.

By mid-September production was now fully in swing, but worries about the state of the cast and crew continued. Production continued even as Monroe fell back into her drug habits and her marriage to Miller disintegrated. The two rarely spoke to each other and there were rumors of the impending divorce.

Location filming ended on October 18 and only a few weeks of interior filming on a Hollywood soundstage was left. When filming concluded on November 5, 1960, the production figures were put at more than $400,000 over budget. The cast and crew were at last relieved to find they had made it through production. It was one of the toughest productions many of them had ever encountered. But the troubles weren't over.

Tragedy Strikes

Gable filmed his final scene on November 2 and told Huston on November 4, "I think this is the best thing I've ever done." He was going to be a father for the first time and added "Now all I want out of life is what Langland [his character in the film] wants — to see that kid of mine born."

A day later, Clark Gable suffered a massive heart attack. The strain of the film and performing his own stunts was said to have played a role in Gable's weakened state. He improved over the next nine days with his wife at his side, but on the 10th day he suddenly died. Gable himself practically predicted it, knowing how tough the production was.

Joan Crawford told writer Roy Newquist that she had received a phone call from Gable during the production and that he told her, "Joan, this picture couldn't be better named. Miller,

Marilyn, Monty Clift — they're all loonies. It's a fucking mess!" Crawford said it was the saddest memory she had after hearing of Gable's death.

Monroe was also distraught. On November 11, it was announced that her marriage to Miller was over and less than a week later Gable's death hit her very hard. Having often imagined him as a father figure she was thrilled to have finally had the chance to work with him. But her behavior on the set put a noticeable strain on Gable and the rest of the production team and Monroe was aware of it. Clark Gable's wife, Kay, was rumored to blame Monroe for his death and that only made Monroe feel worse. She was again near suicide said some of the people close to her.

The Release

As for the film, Huston and Miller continued working on it, but were not as happy with the results. When the film was finally released it did not garner the attention everyone had hoped for. Many reviewers felt the film did not come together. It is true

Montgomery Clift, Marilyn Monroe and Clark Gable

that both Gable and Monroe were praised for their performances, as were many others in the cast, but the film was viewed as a failure at the box office and was the most expensive black and white film ever produced at that time. Final production costs reportedly reached $4 million. Twentieth Century Fox President Spyros Skouras was rumored to have said of the film, "Never has so much talent been wasted."

The New York Times wrote of the film, "Characters and theme do not congeal. There is a lot of absorbing detail in it, but it doesn't add up to a point. Mr. Huston's direction is dynamic, inventive and colorful. Mr. Gable is ironically vital. ... But the picture just doesn't come off."

As for Monroe, her life after this point has been well-chronicled. Hospitalization, drug problems and emotional stress plagued her final years and *The Misfits* was the last film she and Clark Gable ever produced. It was August, 1962 when she died of an overdose.

Today, *The Misfits* is regarded as a classic motion picture. Its stark black and white production and the performances of some of the leading stars of its era proved to be a lasting glimpse of classic movie-making. But the surrounding events of the filming have been one of the lasting factors in keeping the film alive.

Curse of the Silver Screen

Marnie

1964

Tragedy and Disaster Behind the Movies

Obsession Casts a Shadow Over Marnie

Alfred Hitchcock's interest in his leading lady wreaks havoc on the set of his 1964 suspense classic

Known as the Master of Suspense, Alfred Hitchcock's long and popular career as one of Hollywood's best known and most successful directors can hardly be seen as anything but magnificent. His classic motion pictures continue to delight fans and create discussion through books, magazine articles and television. But for Hitchcock, popularity and acclaim were means to acceptance by an insecure man who may never have felt fully comfortable with himself, but only with the world he created on film.

Hitchcock's ordinary looks and his battles with weight never provided him with the handsome good looks of his leading men, but his longing for his leading ladies is evident in many of the director's greatest films and became more evident as his career progressed.

Hitchcock's Leading Lady

In his later years, the image of a cool, beautiful blonde emerged as a central figure in most of his films. Grace Kelly, the quintessential Hitchcock leading lady starred in three of the director's most successful pictures and would have certainly appeared in more had she not married the Prince of Monaco and become Princess Grace. Kim Novak in *Vertigo*, Doris Day in *The Man Who Knew Too Much,* Vera Miles in *The Wrong Man*, Eva Marie Saint in *North By Northwest* and Janet Leigh in *Psycho* all filled that role to some extent, although none captured Hitchcock's eye the way Kelly had. Not until Tippi Hedren.

DALMAS/Sipa Press

Alfred Hitchcock and Tippy Hedren in Cannes, 1963.

In Hedren, Hitchcock saw a beauty that spelled star and an actress he could mold into his replacement for Grace Kelly. She starred in two films for Hitchcock — one of his biggest hits, *The Birds,* and one of his greatest failures, *Marnie.* The plans Hitchcock had for Hedren and the production problems he faced during the making of *Marnie* made for a doomed production that spelled disaster for both director and star and a film that has been examined and reexamined for years for both its impact onscreen and off. Critics and fans alike are still unable to come to a conclusion on the worthiness of *Marnie* within Hitchcock's body of work.

It was the fall of 1961 when Hitchcock first became aware of Tippi Hedren. The director and his wife Alma were reportedly watching the *Today* show one morning when he spotted a beautiful young model in a commercial. She was selling a diet drink called Sego and as she walked across the screen a boy's whistle caused her to stop, turn and smile. Hitchcock became fascinated almost at once.

Later that morning Hitchcock told his agents to find out who the beauty was and by the afternoon he had her name, Natalie Hedren, and a meeting had been arranged. For Hedren, the meeting was with MCA and Hitchcock's name was never mentioned. It wasn't until several days after her first meeting, during a second set of interviews, that his name came up. Hedren eventually met the director, but thought she was being considered for a small role in his popular TV series.

Natalie Hedren had found success as a model in New York when she decided to head to Hollywood to continue modeling and try her hand at commercials. In an interview she said, "I had come to Los Angeles not only to try for better work than what was in New York, but also because I wanted my daughter to grow up in a home with a yard and trees and a neighborhood to roam and play in."

Hedren was a single mother whose four-year-old daughter grew up to be actress Melanie Griffith.

The Director's Biggest Hit

Psycho had been Alfred Hitchcock's most successful film.

Fans flocked to see it and critics ranked it as one of the best films of 1960. To top it, Hitchcock needed a film that had the thrills, scares and suspense he had been long known for, but he needed them in a vehicle that would outshine the success of *Psycho*. He decided on *The Birds*, a roller coaster ride of a thriller as flocks of angry birds attack a small town in northern California. And Natalie Hedren would be introduced to moviegoers as its star after being renamed Tippi Hedren, a nickname she got when she was younger which came from the word Tupsa, a Swedish term of endearment. But Hitchcock actually believed the birds and himself would be the stars of the picture and the unknown beauty would provide the glamour he desired without outshining the special effects that would sell the movie.

Hedren was signed to a seven-year contract and groomed for stardom. The director gave her elaborate screen tests, even bringing in well-known actor Martin Balsam, who had worked with Hitchcock on *Psycho*, to film a test with her. He had a full wardrobe designed for her to wear while working and not working and began molding her into his next Grace Kelly, teaching her how to be his star blonde.

The Birds was a tough film for the director to make and maybe even tougher for its star. Appearing in almost every scene, Hedren was subjected to long hours of takes where birds were tossed at her, tied to her and some even came close to the horror depicted in the film. Special effects did the rest and *The Birds* became Hitchcock's most technically challenging and expensive films.

In the end it paid off. While critics recognized the technical and special effects success, the film was not regarded as highly as *Psycho*. But moviegoers came out in droves and within a month after its opening, the movie had made $11 million. *Psycho*, by comparison had grossed $7 million in its entire first run in U.S. theaters.

Difficult Task of Topping *The Birds*

For a follow-up to *The Birds*, the task again was a daunting one. Hitchcock had been considering a film based on a book by Winston Graham. *Marnie* had actually been viewed as a vehicle for Grace Kelly's return to the big screen. And a statement issued by the Royal Palace in Monaco in March, 1962, said that Princess Grace would "play the lead in Hitchcock's new film *Marnie*." But the public outcry in Monaco was immense and the idea of the princess returning to Hollywood was too much. In addition, the possibility of the princess returning to Hollywood fueled rumors that her fairy tale marriage was in trouble.

Another hitch to the princess' return was that when Kelly left Hollywood for Monaco she still had more than four years left on her MGM contract. And while it was bad publicity for the studio to press that issue while she was in retirement, the idea of her filming for Universal led to threats of possible legal action even though it was announced that her salary would be donated to several children's charities.

Alfred Hitchcock

Princess Grace eventually decided it was best to decline the role and give up the hope of returning to the silver screen. The picture was then put off until Hitchcock found a suitable star. The director was quite disappointed.

After signing Hedren to a seven-year contract at $500 a week and seeing early footage from *The Birds*, Hitchcock decided Hedren would be his next Grace Kelly and her replacement in *Marnie*. She was tested with *The Birds*. Hedren passed the test and the film succeeded for Hitchcock.

By the time *Marnie* began filming Hedren was already worried over the constant supervision of Hitchcock. And during filming, Hitchcock supposedly gave the cameraman instructions to bring the camera as close to Hedren's face as possible, telling the cameraman that the lenses were "almost to make love to the star."

He asked crew members on the set to trail her outside the studio and report back to him her every move, and according to one biographer, he even had her handwriting analyzed to see if there was anything in her personality to show hidden desires for the director which she covered with a coolness. Nothing was found, but Hitchcock's desire for her supposedly grew anyway.

During the same time the director invited studio executives to the set to see what he referred to as his "ultimate actress." Hitchcock believed she was giving an Academy-Award performance and spoke strongly of his feelings for her. "They were not surprised at the feelings," wrote one biographer. "They were astounded at his admission of them."

As the months went on Hedren's frustration and anger grew. The cast and crew knew of the trouble but production continued as if there were no tension. During filming, Hitchcock also began preparations for his next film, called *Mary Rose,* which again would star Hedren. But before *Mary Rose* could be filmed, the tension reached a boiling point and the relationship between director and star took an ugly turn.

Sexual Tension Reaches its Boiling Point

Filming on *Marnie* neared completion and after months of watching her, directing her life on and off the set, and subjecting her to uncomfortable sexual innuendoes, the director finally went too far. Alone in Hedren's trailer after a day of filming, Hitchcock reportedly made a sexual proposition that Hedren could not ignore casually, as she had the director's previous gestures.

Reports say Hedren was shocked by his forwardness and directly refused his advances making it clear to the director she had no intention of ever being sexually involved with him. Hitchcock was furious. Being spurned by her was a blow to his ego.

Some say this exchange never took place. There were rumors that the parting came after Hedren made a comment about the director's weight. Hedren has denied this. She claimed his refusal to allow her to accept a *Photoplay* award on national television for most promising new actress in 1964 caused an angry confrontation between them which resulted in his anger.

First he canceled plans for *Mary Rose*. Then he cut her salary and forever after refused to address the actress personally. He would only call her "that girl."

He would also attempt to ruin her career. She was still under contact but would only be given smaller roles on television. And it even appeared he wanted *Marnie* to fail.

He lost interest in technical details of the film and in the editing process altogether. He refused advice of others on the film to rework some of the rear projection shots and special effects and retreated to his home, occasionally visiting the studio to view footage of the film.

When the film was finally released in 1964 it rated a failure for both Hitchcock and Hedren. *Time* magazine said of the movie "When an unknown director turns out a suspense yarn melodrama as dreary and unconvincing as this, moviegoers reveal the thought of what it might have been if Hitchcock had done it. It is disconcerting to come away from *Marnie* feeling precisely the same way."

Many critics panned the initial release and fans rejected it, expecting a suspense yarn to out-do *The Birds*. Hedren and co-star Sean Connery, were also singled out for their lack-luster performances. The filmed did poorly at the box office and Hitchcock did minimal promotion of the film and gave little support to its star.

Hitchcock handed over her contract to Universal, but when she refused work in a Universal TV series, the contract was reportedly torn up. But by then the damage was done. Hitchcock had refused to allow her to star in a film being produced by Francois Truffaut and his *Mary Rose* project would never be made, with or without Hedren. The roles that were offered were small or in mediocre productions.

Looking Back

Since the 1964 film's release a lot has happened. Hitchcock's TV series had already been canceled and he took several years before creating another film. Of the four that followed, two are listed as failures — *Torn Curtain* and *Topaz* — and two found modest success — *Frenzy* and *Family Plot*. None recaptured the director's glorious past, although *Frenzy,* in 1972, came closest. The director died in 1980 and according to biographer Francios Truffaut, who had a series of interviews with the director in his later years, he refused to discuss his relationship with Tippi Hedren. In addition, after *Marnie,* the image of a cool, beautiful blonde never again appeared in a Hitchcock picture.

In regards to her relationship with Hitchcock, Hedren said in 1994, "An obsession is what it was. It's a very miserable situation to be the object of someone's obsession. It's very confining, very frightening, and I didn't like it."

Hedren married and raised her daughter, who became a successful actress as well — Melanie Griffith. Hedren also occasionally worked in television and film. Her films include *A Countess From Hong Kong, Pacific Heights,* and *Through the Eyes of a Killer.* She has also been active on television with roles in several TV movies, a role on the cable series *Dream On* and in the soap opera *The Bold and the Beautiful.* In addition, she returned for a cable-made sequel to Hitchcock's *The Birds.*

Tippi Hedren today

But Hedren's largest accomplishment since her work with Hitchcock has been the development of Shambala Preserve, a 60-acre ranch in Acton, California where some 68 large animals, including leopards, mountain lions, Bengal and Siberian tigers, African lions and African elephants roam free. Hedren has been honored with numerous awards for her efforts and uses her celebrity to raise awareness of the treatment of endangered species and her film work helps support the preserve financially. The preserve itself came about after Hedren filmed the movie *Roar* in Soledad

Canyon and developed the preserve to provide a home for some of the animals used in the film. It's ironic that her movie debut in *The Birds* had her being menaced by savage gulls and crows, considering her later dedication to the protection of wild creatures.

Of Hitchcock, Hedren said in an interview, "I've seen most of Hitch's movies and I've read some biographies, but I'm not sure I ever knew the real Hitchcock. Perhaps no one did."

It's important to mention that not everyone supports a theory of Hitchcock obsessed with his leading ladies. Two of his other leading ladies — Kim Novak and Janet Leigh — have both publicly stated that they never saw that side of the director when they worked with him. Leigh never found the director as anything but professional and Novak, characterized her working with Hitchcock as "a wonderful experience" during *Vertigo*.

As for *Marnie*, much has been written and said. While still not regarded as Hitchcock's greatest accomplishment, some regard it as the director's most personal film, with its troubled sexual themes and dual personalities. *Marnie* has been reevaluated for its rich vision and deep story, filled with turmoil and mystery that seems all the more interesting knowing the circumstances under which it was created.

In 1986, on the release of the film to video, *The Chicago Tribune* wrote, "*Marnie*, with its astonishingly naked, vulnerable performance by Tippi Hedren, is also the most emotionally open of Hitchcock's films ... A dense, beautiful film, it well rewards the multiple viewings made possible by home video."

Tragedy and Disaster Behind the Movies

Cleopatra

1963

Tragedy and Disaster Behind the Movies

A Costly *Cleopatra*

***Burton and Taylor love affair
and massive production woes
bring studio to brink of ruin***

If there ever was a doomed production it was the filming the Twentieth Century Fox epic *Cleopatra*. It's hard to imagine a production filled with more turmoil and with more disruption in the history of filmmaking. *Cleopatra* stands out as one of the most difficult of film productions.

It's not so much that *Cleopatra* is a bad film, but the cost of the production and the results delivered, while both lavish, wreaked havoc on those that played a part in the movie and even some who did not.

Originally filmed in 1917 starring actress Theda Bara, then remade in 1934 with Claudette Colbert, Fox decided the story was due for a remake. Actually, there had been work on a remake, but it wasn't until the head of Fox, Spyros Skouras, saw early scenes of the epic *Ben-Hur* that sold him on the idea of an updated, but lavish *Cleopatra*.

A Remake in Production is Axed

The remake version, already in pre-production, was a low-budget film starring Joan Collins as Cleopatra, Peter Finch as Julius Caesar and Stephen Boyd as Mark Antony. The early version was budgeted at a paltry $210,000, but when a larger version was put into production, the cast was altered and the budget was increased to $5 million.

There were numerous actresses vying for the role of Cleopatra. After Joan Collins was cut out of the deal, five leading ladies were in the running for the role — Joanne Woodward, Marilyn Monroe, Brigitte Bardot, Gina Lollobrigida and Elizabeth Taylor. Soon the names were cut down to two: Lollobrigida and Taylor. After viewing the work of both actresses, Skouras chose Lollobrigida.

Elizabeth Taylor as Cleopatra

The studio's only worry was that the Italian actress, who was better known as a bombshell than as an actress, might not be a big enough name to sell the expensive picture, so Skouras polled U.S. motion picture exhibitors and they responded overwhelmingly that Taylor was the bigger draw. Taylor got the role. Her salary was approximately $2 million by the time the picture was in theaters. She received $125,000 for the first 16 weeks of filming,

$50,000 each week after, and 10 percent of the gross profits, along with $3,000 a week in living expenses. The salary was nearly half the film's initial budget. Both Peter Finch and Stephen Boyd were retained from the earlier version at salaries significantly lower than Taylor's.

The first hitch in filming came when Taylor had to film one more role for MGM before she was allowed to take the role of Cleopatra. The film was *Butterfield 8* and the production of *Cleopatra* was delayed. Taylor was originally set for the role in *Cleopatra* in early 1959, but filming didn't commence until late 1960. By that point Taylor reportedly called for a new director, Rouben Mamoulian was out and Joseph Mankiewicz was in. Some reports say Mamoulian resigned from the project rather that deal with Taylor's antics.

Also out were co-stars Finch and Boyd. Taylor asked that friend Rex Harrison portray Caesar and suggested Richard Burton for the role of Antony. Burton had to be bought out of his contract for *Camelot*, which was currently on stage, at a cost of $50,000. As it turned out, Fox could have saved the money because Burton's *Camelot* contract was up in the summer of 1961 and Burton never filmed a scene of *Cleopatra* until the beginning of 1962. But Fox had no idea of the fate falling on *Cleopatra*.

Location shooting was to take place in Britain. The original film's sets in Hollywood were not expansive enough and new sets were constructed in London at a cost of $3 million. Production was finally ready to begin when Taylor came down with cold and became sick and feverish. She reportedly developed meningitis and the crew tried to shoot around her absence, but that was nearly impossible since the script had her in almost every scene. In addition, the cold weather not only made the actress sick, but the eight-and-a-half acres of palm trees flown in for the shooting died in the cold, dreary weather and had to be replaced.

In March 1961, Taylor developed an abscessed tooth and then a spinal irritation that kept her from filming. And before she could film even one minute of footage she developed pneumonia and a congestion in her lungs put her near death. When she stopped breathing, an emergency tracheotomy saved her life, but the film would again be delayed. It was decided Taylor could not film in damp London and production was halted.

Taylor returned to the Hollywood to recuperate and filming was delayed until fall, 1961. Location shooting was moved to Rome, a warmer climate for the star to work in. The sets in London were dismantled and sold. At this stage there were less than 8 minutes of footage captured on film and the budget had topped $8 million. The studio was worrying.

A New Beginning in Rome

New sets were constructed in Rome at a cost of $5.5 million and the script was also tossed out and had to be rewritten adding more money to the now $15 million budget. Further escalating things, Taylor demanded the film be shot in Todd A-O, the wide-screen format created by her late husband Mike Todd. This added another $10 million to the cost of *Cleopatra*. Now the budget was passing $25 million.

When filming did finally begin to move along other costs came into play. Taylor's husband, Eddie Fisher, was signed on as a production assistant even though there was no idea what he would do. He was paid $150,000.

Taylor's other demands during production also escalated costs. Fox supplied her with several Rolls-Royces for transportation, she had her doctor paid for and kept him by her side throughout the filming. There were cooks and butlers, imported china and wine, as well as hairstylists and a secretarial staff. Orders from local groceries stores were delivered each day to her Rome palace at a cost of some $150 a day. It has been written that her liquor bill during the filming topped $500 a week.

Other delays plagued the filming, including strikes from the hairdressers, a group of Italian technicians, and a cast of Cleopatra's handmaidens, who claimed they were being pinched and sexually harassed by male extras. Another story of a cat that gave birth to kittens under a set reportedly cost production $17,000 as a crew dismantled the set to remove the animals only then to rebuild it so filming could resume.

Another Husband on the Horizon

In 1959, Taylor and Fisher were very much in love. He had left wife Debbie Reynolds to comfort Taylor after the death of her husband, Mike Todd and soon the two fell in love and married. By 1962 the tables were turning.

By the middle of 1961 the marriage was already shaky. Taylor was no longer reeling from the death of her previous husband and her clout in Hollywood was ever increasing and she enjoyed this form of new-found freedom as well as an Academy Award for Best Actress in *Butterfield 8*. Fisher himself was said to be growing tired of being known as "Mr. Elizabeth Taylor" and even the title didn't get him the work he desired. His work mainly consisted of a role in his wife's last film and a production assistant on her latest work. In walked Richard Burton and Fisher's days were numbered. Burton and Taylor began an affair during the filming of

Liz Taylor and Richard Burton

Cleopatra and their stormy relationship has been well chronicled. Richard Burton's marriage also suffered during filming of *Cleopatra*, eventually ending in divorce.

Their relationship was a stormy one and during production it heated up and cooled off leaving cast and crew to wonder if a stormy end to the romance would cause an immediate and costly end to the film. Publicity managers on the film reported that the romantic relationship developing on the set had the entire cast and crew, except for Taylor and Burton, in knots. And the worries about what the Taylor-Burton relationship would do to the film's release consumed studio executives. Fox had created an image of family-oriented pictures and the bad publicity of an affair between the stars and their impending divorces could spell box office disaster. The studio tried to keep a lid on the rumors for as long as possible. The cost of production continued to escalate adding to the executives' worries. In time its effects were felt by many outside the film's production.

Fox Faces Money Woes

Twentieth Century Fox was near bankruptcy. The cost of *Cleopatra* nearly broke the studio. To pay the production cost, the studio sold off its back lots, mortgaged all its corporate property and cut everywhere it could to make ends meet. By the time filming began in Rome only one other major Fox film was in production. It was Marilyn Monroe's *Something's Got To Give*. The film was never finished. Monroe was fired from the production, but then was set to step back into the role when she died of a drug overdose in August, 1962.

The cost of *Cleopatra* ripped through the production of *Something's Got To Give*. Location shooting was nixed to save money and an elaborate dream sequence was cut because of costs. Even Monroe's salary was a paltry sum of $100,000, due to an old contract she had with Fox, compared to Taylor's million-dollar salary. In addition, the fact the she didn't get the role of Cleopatra angered Monroe, who was Fox's leading money-maker, while Taylor was on loan from MGM.

Fox had traveled so deeply into the hole that the only way they could redeem themselves was to finish the picture and get it released to make back the cost. It had hoped that both *Something's Got to Give* and *Cleopatra* turned out to be big money-makers and the inexpensive picture and the costly epic would balance out and show a profit to the studio. *Something's Got To Give* never made it to theaters and the results of the *Cleopatra* never proved to be the success the studio had so hoped for.

While filming on *Cleopatra* continued, costs moved skyward. More than a million dollars was added when the film was shot in chronological order and actors sat around for weeks collecting salaries between takes that could have been done back to back and were instead placed weeks apart. Production reports showed that Richard Burton worked just five times in the first 17 weeks of the production and actor Carroll O'Conner collected a salary for 14 weeks while waiting to film just two close-ups.

In addition, theft was a problem on the set. Sets were built on overtime and then gathered dust while waiting to be used or were never used. Swords and other articles on the set were stolen and had to be replaced, and massive food bills and catered lunches were charged for food that was reportedly already purchased by the film studio. All in all the budget had creeped passed $30 million to become the costliest production to date.

The Movie is Completed

In 1962 Darryl Zanuck was brought into Fox as the company's president to help the studio out of its major financial woes, replacing Spyros Skouras. Zanuck managed to push production along and force the film to finish in hopes of salvaging the studio.

Final production totals for *Cleopatra* vary. The final tally on the budget for the film was reported at $38 million, yet some reports say the film actually cost more than $44 million to finish. By today's standards the film has been estimated at a cost of roughly $220 million.

While Taylor made plenty of money off the film, the box office receipts only totaled $26 million. Therefore, even with a conservative budget figure, the film lost some $12 million.

And even in today's big-budget productions, *Cleopatra* is still considered the costliest movie ever made and Fox's hope of making the greatest epic of all

Elizabeth Taylor

time fell short with mediocre reviews. The offscreen publicity of the romance between Taylor and Burton and the stories of the lavish production were the main reasons audiences were drawn to the picture.

Reviews said Taylor's acting was bad and said the film shows the strain under which it was made. The box office receipts would have been strong had the film not cost so much to produce and Fox barely made it out of the deal. It wasn't until 1965 and the release of *The Sound of Music* that the studio began its turnaround. Taylor and Burton continued successful careers, but their onscreen union only resulted in the destruction of both their current marriages and they tried unsuccessfully twice at marriage to each other. Their offscreen images long outlived their debacle of *Cleopatra*.

The stars of the picture in an ad for the film.

Rebel Without A Cause

1955

Tragedy and Disaster Behind the Movies

Doomed Rebels

A trio of young stars create movie history and are each plagued by tragic deaths while still very young

For three young stars it was a film that would make them cultural icons. One forever etched in our minds as a legend and a myth. Another forever remembered as the troubled youth he created onscreen. And the third, a young woman who would go on to great things, but would always be remembered for her role in this screen classic.

The 1955 Cinemascope classic by Warner Bros., *Rebel Without a Cause,* struck a chord with a generation of teens and forever sealed the images of James Dean, Sal Mineo and Natalie Wood in the minds of the American public as troubled youths searching for the answers.

This classic motion picture has stood the test of time and continues to draw crowds at revivals every time it reappears on theater screens. But in addition to the angst depicted by the actors onscreen, the three young stars were linked by a series of tragic accidents taking each of their lives while still very young and looking to bright and successful futures.

Dean shot to stardom after the release of his first movie, Elia Kazan's *East of Eden*, based on the John Steinbeck novel. He had appeared on Broadway and in television and was known throughout Hollywood circles as a talented young man destined for stardom, but he came across as sometimes rude and most times standoffish. Regardless of his behavior, Warner Bros. signed him to a contract for *East of Eden* and soon saw a star in the making. Before the movie was even released he was scheduled to make *Rebel Without a Cause*.

The Book Becomes a Movie

Warner Bros. bought the rights to a book by Robert Lindner called *Rebel Without a Cause* in 1946 and within a year was preparing a screenplay to film the story of a group of troubled juvenile delinquents. Marlon Brando was set for the leading role, but the screenplay was reportedly unusable and the film was never made.

James Dean

Director Nicholas Ray appeared at Warner Bros. several years later wanting to make a film about juvenile delinquency. And after success with his western *Johnny Guitar*, Warner Bros. was thrilled to have the director take up residence as a director on the studio lot. And since Warners owned the rights to the book Ray decided the story would be his next project.

Ray took the title from the original screenplay, but little

else, setting off to do his own screenplay. First, using Warners' writer Leon Uris for the project and then Irving Shulman, Ray found it difficult to get the screenplay he wanted written.

By the beginning of 1955 no acceptable screenplay had been developed and Ray was growing frustrated. But fortunately Ray attended a party where he met a writer named Stewart Stern. The two ended up in a discussion of Ray's problems with the story and Ray asked Stern if he was interested in working on the screenplay. Stern accepted. A successful screenplay was soon developed.

The screenplay tells the story of a group of troubled teens over a 24-hour period. Jim Stark, the leading character, is drunk in the street as dawn approaches and the sound of a siren wails in the distance. Next he's at a police station where he comes in contact with the other leading characters in the film. A young girl, Judy, and a boy, Plato, have also been picked up for criminal mischief. A police detective tries to reach out to the youths and come to the bottom of their troubles, but they resist believing all adults incapable of comprehending their struggles.

The next day the teens meet again on their way to school. Jim Stark is facing his first day at the new school and later that afternoon crosses a gang of boys during a school trip to the planetarium. They challenge him to a car race, or a "chickie run" in which two cars race towards the edge of a cliff and the first to jump from the car before going over the edge of the cliff is the loser. The gang leader, who happens to be Judy's boyfriend, is killed in the car race when he gets caught inside as the car heads over a cliff and the three teens are once again drawn together.

The remaining gang members want revenge against Stark and the trio hides out in a deserted mansion. Eventually they end up back at the planetarium where police show up and Plato is killed when they believe he's got a gun.

In late March, 1955 the movie was scheduled to begin filming, but first a cast had to be chosen. Much of the gang members were chosen with the help of Dean. The star tested with many of them and several were chosen because they had worked with him before. Ray thought this would help the actors perform better as a gang if they were already on familiar terms.

For the role of Plato, Dean wanted the role to go to another friend of his. Reports say Dean wanted his friend Jack Simmons to play the part, but Ray didn't think he was right for the role. Plato was to be a 15-year-old boy whose parents had no interest in him and were usually off traveling. Plato longed for a father and mother figure and Jim and Judy filled those roles in his eyes. Sal Mineo was one of the many who showed up during casting calls and Ray felt his small appearance and large, sad eyes made him right for the role. But the real test was his chemistry with Dean.

A test was held and the two actors read through a scene but initially failed to connect. Ray then suggested the actors sit and talk for a while, hoping it would relax Mineo enough to try again. During the conversation Dean discovered that Mineo was from the Bronx and soon the two were talking at length about New York. Next they moved onto the subject of cars and soon a definite rapport had been established. A short time later Sal Mineo was signed to the role of Plato.

For the pivotal role of Judy, Dean again suggested a friend of his — Christine White. In addition to White, several other actresses were considered including Debbie Reynolds, Lori Nelson and Jayne Mansfield. But in the end it was 16-year-old Natalie Wood that got the part. The cast rounded out with veteran actors Jim Backus and Ann Doran filling the roles of Jim's parents.

Surprisingly enough, Dean wasn't the studio's first choice for the lead role either. Tab Hunter was what Warner Bros. pictured originally. But Ray had other ideas in mind and Dean got the part that made him a legend.

Because a number of the actors were underage, California law restricted the underage actors from working for more than four hours and required Hollywood studios to have a tutor on the set for four hours of education making filming an additional challenge.

The director felt strongly about a cohesive cast and encouraged the actors to spend time together on and off the set so their screen performances would look comfortable and natural. Natalie Wood's sister Lana, confirmed the stars' friendship. "She [Natalie] remained friends with Nicholas Ray, the director, and for many years she was close to her co-stars Nick Adams and Sal

Mineo. She also had a brief and intense friendship with Jimmy Dean who spent most of his time away from the filming with her," recalled Wood. "Nick, Sal and Jimmy were often at our home, sitting out around the pool, eating, laughing and playing games."

An LA Backdrop

Filming began on March 28th with most of the production shot on location in the Los Angeles area. Santa Monica High School, the D.W. Griffith Observatory and the Hollywood jail served as key locations. And while production continued on schedule, Dean was known to hold up cast and crew during filming. Before one scene Dean kept the entire cast and crew waiting for nearly an hour as he sat in his dressing room, drinking wine and playing a set of drums. When the actor was ready to perform, he marched immediately onto the set, and captured a lengthy seven-minute scene on the first take.

Natalie Wood and James Dean

And while cast and crew soon had faith in Dean's ability as an actor, the bosses at Warner Bros. had their doubts. Studio executives didn't like what they saw in the dailies and ordered the production brought to a halt. Ray was reportedly summoned to Jack Warner's office.

"Take me off salary and sell me all the rights to the film," was Nick Ray's response to Warner when questioned about his film. The studio executives said they'd consider the option. But after checking with projectionist on the film, they changed their minds. "Frankly, I think it's the only picture worth anything on the lot," the projectionist reported when asked what he thought of the film. Warner Bros. backed down and production resumed. Filming went on as scheduled and wrapped up at the end of May.

The projectionist was right. *Rebel Without a Cause* would turn out to be one of Warner's greatest motion pictures and one the biggest hits of 1955. But tragedy had already begun taking its toll on the stars.

Dean's Love of Racing

Immediately after finishing *Rebel*, Dean began filming *Giant* with Elizabeth Taylor and Rock Hudson. Dean's co-star from *Rebel*, Sal Mineo, even had a small part in the production.

One of Dean's favorite pastimes was racing. During production of *Rebel*, an opportunity arose and Dean headed off to race his car, winning two trophies, while another driver that day lost his life in a crash. Director of *Giant,* George Stevens had no intention of jeopardizing his movie and support the star's love of racing. During *Giant*, Dean was forbidden to race or to take his Porsche to Texas during location shooting.

Dean raced anyway and barely avoided a serious crash after production on the film had begun, but Dean was not needed on the set yet. Dean reported to location shooting in Texas in early June and returned in July to continue the film in Hollywood.

By August early word on *Rebel* was that the film was magnificent and Dean's performance was top notch. The movie was previewed in mid-September and Dean knew it would be a hit. Anxious to finish *Giant* and race again, Dean traded in his old Porsche for a newer Porsche 550 Spyder and began planning for an October race in Salinas, California. Along with the new car, Dean purchased a life insurance policy for $100,000.

As Dean raced around town in his new Porsche, friends began fearing his safety. Henry Ginsberg, co-producer on *Giant,* accepted an offer from Dean for a ride in his car and returned to the studio telling the production department "If you have any loose ends you better tie them up quick. The way this kid's handling that car I don't think he's going to be around much longer."

Dean finished work on *Giant* a few days later and that weekend headed off to race in Salinas. Dean drove the car with a mechanic along for the ride. Dean received a speeding ticket for going 65 mph in a 45 mph zone. A short time later the car crashed into a Ford truck. The mechanic was thrown 19 feet on impact, but later recovered. Dean broke his neck and was crushed by the steering wheel. Reports say he died instantly.

Rebel Without a Cause was released and became an instant hit and a classic. Dean's death ironically added to the image the film created and fans flocked to movie screens to see the movie. And according to reports, in the three years following his death, Dean received more fan mail than any living star. There were even rumors the actor was alive and hiding. The crushed Porsche was later exhibited, but has since vanished and no one seems to know where the car is today.

The remaining cast of *Rebel* was shattered by the death of their co-star and friend, even though some saw it coming. Frank Mazzola, one of the gang members in the film recalled Dean giving him a ride in his car during the filming. "I swear to God, it was like I was going to die," Mazzola recalled in an interview. "He would go as fast as he could around blind curves, and he'd go into oncoming traffic as if it wasn't there."

Sal Mineo in the 70s.

Tragedy Follows Surviving Stars

For Sal Mineo, Dean's death struck a rough blow. He and Dean had been close during the filming and Mineo also had a small role in *Giant* and the loss of his friend was hard. Mineo was nominated for an Academy Award for his role in *Rebel*, but didn't win the Oscar. He continued working and was again nominated for his role in *Exodus* a few years later. But as the decade came to a close Mineo outgrew his troubled youth image. The 1960s offered him little in the way of dramatic roles and parts were few and far between. In the mid 60s he had a role in a smaller cult film called *Who Killed Teddy Bear?*, but mostly TV crime and detective dramas, such as *Columbo,* were the only vehicles that offered him roles.

In the mid-70s, after his Hollywood-style spending left him broke, he returned to the stage and began to turn his career around as a producer. But the turnaround was short lived and on February 13, 1976 Mineo was mysteriously stabbed to death outside his West Hollywood apartment. He was returning from a play rehearsal of "P.S. Your Cat is Dead" when he was attacked after he got out of his car and headed toward his apartment. Bystanders later saw a man fleeing the scene, but it took more than two years to uncover his killer. Lionel R. Williams, a convicted killer was reportedly overheard detailing his killing of Mineo while serving time in a Michigan jail. Witnesses reported the killer as a white male, possibly with long blond hair. Since Williams was black he was initially discarded as a suspect. But Williams' wife reportedly told police he came home that evening and was covered in blood saying he had just killed a man in Hollywood. The trial proved that Williams had long auburn-colored hair at the time of the killing and because of the darkness his skin color would not have been visible. He was also suspected of a number of other robberies in the area at the same time. He was convicted of second-degree murder in 1979.

Mineo was only 37 and his tragic death added another layer to the cult favorite that now had two young stars frozen onscreen.

Natalie Wood made it a trio when she tragically drowned off Catalina Island in 1981. Wood's career was a long and successful one. She, like Mineo, had also been nominated twice for Academy Awards, but never won. She was currently working on a film called *Brainstorm,* in 1981, when she and husband Robert Wagner took off for a weekend on their boat the *Splendor* along with Wood's current co-star, Christopher Walken.

Wood was always terribly frightened of water, according to her sister, but for unknown reasons she went out on deck late one evening. Reports suggest she may have had trouble sleeping because of a dingy pounding against the side of the boat. She may have gone out to tie the small boat down when she slipped and fell overboard, hitting her head and drowning. She was only 43. Wood's final performance was reworked for *Brainstorm* because at the time of her death she still had several key scenes to film. The script was written around the tragedy and the film was released after her death, but earned mediocre reviews and did little at the box office except to draw fans to her last screen performance.

Today, *Rebel Without a Cause* is a cult classic. Images of the film stand out as much for its artful direction and its breakthrough imagery of troubled youth in a suppressed 1950s as it does for the tragedies that befell the trio of stars that helped make the movie a classic in the first place.

Natalie Wood

Tragedy and Disaster Behind the Movies

Raintree County

1957

Tragedy and Disaster Behind the Movies

Tragedy Hits
Raintree County

Montgomery Clift and Elizabeth Taylor star in a drama cursed long before production began

    aintree County was supposed to be Metro-Goldwyn-Mayer's second *Gone With The Wind*. The epic film would feature the look, feel and direction of the famous classic motion picture and, hopefully, reap the profits of its predecessor. The comparisons end there. *Raintree County* proved to be a far different motion picture. The production and the final result differed greatly from the 1939 Academy Award-winning classic.

    It was 1956 when Montgomery Clift and Elizabeth Taylor signed to do the MGM film. For Taylor, it was one of a number of pictures she was to star in, which was part of a long-term relationship with MGM, while for Clift it was the first of a three-picture deal with the studio. He originally didn't want to do the film, but an offer of $300,000, top billing, and a chance to work with Taylor again made him reconsider.

Clift and Taylor thrilled audiences and captured box office receipts in two earlier outings — *A Place in the Sun* gave them both matinee-idol status and *Suddenly Last Summer* gave each a chance to stretch as actors with meatier roles in the heavy drama. *Raintree County* was planned to make them legends of the silver screen, cut from the cloth of Clark Gable and Vivien Leigh.

A Successful Novel Brings Tragic Results

The 1,066-page novel by Ross Lockridge captures sensitive, striking characters facing destructive times at the outset of the Civil War as a young man from Indiana searches for his roots. Madness and desperation, along with a sprawling backdrop,

Elizabeth Taylor and Montgomery Clift in a scene from the 1957 film.

made the story perfect for the big screen. So, when Lockridge's book became a bestseller in 1947 its author became famous and MGM quickly bought the rights for $150,000 and announced plans for the film. The announcement made the book even more popular, but for the author, the success wasn't enough. Or maybe it was too much.

Ross Lockridge was reportedly suffering from depression over editorial cuts made to the book when he told his wife he was going to the post office one day. He went into the garage and turned on the car ignition, attached a vacuum cleaner hose to the exhaust, and committed suicide by carbon monoxide poisoning.

The tragedy, along with a disappointing original screenplay, caused Dore Schary, head of MGM, to shelve plans for the filming. It was decided that the film would be far too costly to bring to the big screen.

The Film Comes Back to Life

The story goes that seven years later, by chance, the idea of the film was resurrected when Millard Kaufman, a young writer at the studio, who was pulled off a movie he was working on, ran screaming into the office of the head of the studio's story department, Ken McKenna. Trying to calm Kaufman down, McKenna grabbed a book off his bookshelf and told Kaufman to go home and read the book while the studio paid him. McKenna had no idea he had given him *Raintree County*. Several days later Kaufman returned to McKenna telling him he wanted to help write the movie version. A screenplay soon followed.

Schary liked the screenplay and the film idea came back to life. The original budget was just over $5 million with shooting in Hollywood and three locations — Mississippi, Tennessee and Kentucky. The film would also introduce Camera65, a new revolutionary wide-screen film process.

Clift supposedly enjoyed Lockridge's book a great deal, but felt the script was "just good enough." At 206 pages, it was clocked at approximately three-and-a-half hours long and was crafted as a soap opera. The actor was said to feel that only first-rate performances by the stars and a strong direction could bring the story to life and make it more than a standard soap opera.

With that assessment, the choice of director would be imperative. MGM originally considered William Wyler and Richard Brooks, but decided on Edward Dmytryk. Whether it was availability or cost, the choice was considered an odd one. Dymtryk, while a capable director, was known mostly for action films like *The Caine Mutiny*. He was not thought of as a director of films with complex characters and emotions, an important factor in successfully bringing *Raintree County* to the big screen.

Filming began in April, 1956 and started off strong with Clift performing in peak form. Clift had prepared for the role with intense work, say his biographers, and he captured his character, John Shawnessy, perfectly.

But Clift was still in trouble. By this point in his career he had trouble dealing with fame and his own success. Drugs and alcohol were a part of his daily existence, using them to enable him to perform became a science. And while it worked for some time, the film's crew began to hear Clift complaining of a lack of sleep and headaches. His odd behavior created suspicion on the set, and the cast and crew noticed that when Clift was on the set his gray bag of drugs was always nearby.

Production Finds Trouble Off the Set

On May 12, Elizabeth Taylor had a party at the Benedict Canyon home she shared with her husband Michael Wilding. Hidden in the hills, twisting, narrow roads, shrouded by trees and shrubs, led to the house and Clift was one of the key guests at the party that evening. In fact, Clift originally declined to attend the party, but at Taylor's pleading he finally agreed to make an appearance.

In addition to Rock Hudson, Kevin McCarthy and the Wildings, Clift attended and drank several glasses of wine that night. He also reportedly took some drugs to relax himself, hoping to getting some rest later that evening, because of trouble he was having sleeping at night.

At about 12:30 am Clift left the party to drive home. Actor Kevin McCarthy left at the same time and agreed to lead the way down the winding roads, showing Clift the way home. McCarthy tells his version of what happened next.

"We started down the hill and all of a sudden he was coming up very fast behind me," McCarthy said. "We were approaching the first turn in the road, and it was very sharp. I didn't know why he was coming up behind me so fast. At the time I thought it was a prank, since I knew he loved to pull things like that. His lights were getting brighter and I thought he was going to hit me and I was going to go right through the house, which was on the hill just beyond the turn, and off the cliff! I turned quickly ... At the next turn, I figured I had had it and I wasn't going to get involved any more in the game."

McCarthy said he sped up and saw Clift driving erratically then, "suddenly his car just wasn't there anymore."

Clift's car flew off the road and hit a telephone pole, bounced off and crashed onto a cliff. He was nearly killed. Party guests were the first to arrive at the scene. They thought Clift was dead. Taylor climbed into the car and held Clift until an ambulance arrived. The actor even lost two of his teeth which became lodged in his throat. Taylor, it's been said, reached into Clift's mouth and pulled the teeth from his throat saving his life.

A newspaper ad for the film.

Reports of the crash made newspapers across the country. But the studio downplayed the crash, never disclosing how serious Clift's condition was.

In reality, Clift suffered a serious concussion, countless cuts and bruises on his face with a serious gash through the middle of his upper lip. He had also lost his front teeth, broken his nose, his jaw, cheekbone and sinus area.

Fortunately the studio had insured Clift to the tune of $500,000 — $450,000 of which was paid to the studio as compensation for expenses Clift's recovery cost the studio due to the accident. Salaries to cast and crew were paid during his recovery and the insurance kept the production afloat. Ironically, this was the first time MGM had ever taken out insurance money on a film in case of injury to its stars. The studio's reasoning had been that Clift's use of drugs and alcohol was well enough known throughout Hollywood that studio executives feared he might not be able to make it through the entire film.

Production on *Raintree County* was shut down for nine weeks while Clift recovered. The studio wondered if they could finish the film and even considered replacing Clift, but with half of the production completed, and more than $2 million spent, it would be nearly impossible to reshoot. It was also feared that removing Clift from the film would be a severe blow to him personally and executives and his co-star Taylor feared he might kill himself if his role was recast.

During this time another problem took shape. Elizabeth Taylor's marriage to Michael Wilding fell apart and their separation was publicly announced the day before she headed to Kentucky to begin shooting the film again. During the weeks when filming was shut down she became involved with producer Mike Todd, whose interest in her became widely publicized.

Back Before the Cameras

Filming resumed on July 23rd with Clift and Taylor on location in Mississippi and then on to Kentucky. Todd pursued Taylor during her time on location, even using Clift to get to her. Clift gave her a pearl ring on the set from Todd along with a message that a real engagement ring was to come later. Taylor's offscreen soap opera was as dramatic as was her onscreen persona's.

For Clift, returning to the film was frightening. His emotional state was even shakier than before the crash. And although most of his injuries had healed, there was still considerable pain and swelling and a change in his appearance, but Clift's own insecurity compounded the problem as he believed his handsome image was destroyed by the crash. Clift's drug-taking and drinking became even heavier after the accident. Clift's performance changed after the accident some reported, saying the actor had to struggle even more to perform and that the drugs were now not used only to help him perform, but to simply allow him to get through the day. It took longer and more and more takes to get the scenes filmed and the entire crew felt the strain.

Some say Dmytryk failed to take control of the situation which made matters worse. When the actors began demanding changes, and the director allowed them, the film began to lose shape.

The cast and crew returned to Hollywood in October, 1956 and it was announced Taylor was filing for divorce from Wilding. And by the time filming wrapped up, Clift believed his career was over. Publicity surrounded the stars' private lives.

The Release

When the film was released in 1957 it had cost almost $5.5 million and was the most expensive picture MGM had filmed in the United States to date. Its box office receipts reached $6 million, so the studio did see a small profit from the picture, but far from the expectations of another *Gone With The Wind*. By comparison, *Gone With the Wind* cost roughly $4 million in 1939 and earned somewhere in the neighborhood of $31 million in first run and rereleases due to its immense popularity. *Raintree County* ranks as the 52nd most successful film of the decade, tied with *Ivanhoe, I'll Cry Tomorrow, North by Northwest* and *Butterfield 8*, all of which brought in $6 million but cost considerably less to make.

The film made little impact at theaters when it was released in 1957 and probably got lost in the shuffle of so many noteworthy films. *The Bridge on the River Kwai* and *Giant* were the big successes, along with *Jailhouse Rock* and *Twelve Angry Men*. *Raintree County* didn't draw the money or the acclaim it was shooting for. Reviewers panned the film and called it a "three-hour bore" and the only real money came from moviegoers who headed to the theater to see Montgomery Clift before and after the crash that nearly took his life.

Before and After

Fans tried to spot the scenes filmed before the crash and noted the scenes after, where Clift's face showed signs of change. In reality, some close to the film say it's hard to tell the difference. Drugs had already taken their toll on Clift's look and performance and some of the scenes fans were sure were filmed after the crash were actually filmed prior to it. The reality was that Clift had not appeared onscreen since 1954 in *From Here To Eternity* and that the three years of drugs and alcohol had taken their toll on his look and performance.

But others say there was a definite change in Clift's look after the crash and to compensate for it, the producers attempted to soften the view and to not film his face directly. And because the left side of his face was still partially swollen and nerve damage made it somewhat immobile, director Dmytryk attempted to film Clift in long shots or from his right profile which hadn't been as badly damaged by the crash.

Ironically, the film was shown in MGM's new Camera65 film process which was heralded as the "Window of the World" process, giving the sharpest image possible making every feature of Clift's face that much more vivid.

Curse of the Silver Screen

The Conqueror

1953

Tragedy and Disaster Behind the Movies

Tragedy Stalks the Stars of *The Conqueror*

John Wayne, Susan Hayward and others face an unknown danger on the set of Howard Hughes' failed epic

When Howard Hughes decided to move forward with the production of an epic about Genghis Khan, who better to play the life of the 12th-Century warrior than the silver screen's biggest hero of them all — John Wayne. But the story of *The Conqueror* was far more shocking offscreen than what the cameras captured. In the end it was more of a horror than an epic.

It was 1954 when Hughes decided that the vast open spaces of Utah, with wide vistas, striking deserts and a timeless atmosphere, would serve as the best backdrop for what Hughes hoped might be a cinematic masterpiece. The fact that atomic

Tragedy and Disaster Behind the Movies

testing had and was still taking place nearby provided no threat to cast and crew according to government reports. But looking back it's hard to imagine how they could not consider the danger involved.

The government reported that there was no risk to residents or visitors to areas located near atomic testing. Even today it's nearly impossible to uncover the whole story behind the dangers the film crew, and anyone who happened to live in the area, faced and for years the government stood by its story that testing posed no danger to cast and crew.

Startling facts

Over the years some startling facts have been revealed, yet the Atomic Energy Commission stood by their story that there was no danger to those living near bomb testing sites in Nevada and Utah. For 12 years, from 1951 to 1963, atomic testing continued and the sparsely populated areas faced a danger unknown to most everyone. The dangers are covered and hidden and the effects were cast off because of lack of evidence that the bombings caused the problems.

Wayne and Hayward in a scene from 'The Conqueror.'

As for the movie, it was to be Hughes' greatest achievement. Hughes began purchasing stock in RKO Studios as far back as 1948 and began testing the waters of Hollywood. He bought controlling rights to RKO in March of 1954 at a cost of about $23.5 million and soon after set forth in planning his epic.

For the filming of *The Conqueror*, the talent of a well-known, leading actor was needed to make the movie top notch. John Wayne wasn't the first choice for the role of Ghengis Kahn. Marlon Brando, it's been reported, was the first choice. Brando was under contract with Twentieth Century Fox at the time and Hughes hoped to get him on loan, but before filming could begin Brando was put on suspension by Fox and was unable to take the part.

Wayne saw a treatment for the film and decided it might be a good vehicle to showcase his acting ability. Even though a huge star, Wayne was rarely recognized for his acting ability and longed to be seen as a serious actor.

Some Wayne biographers say he never picked up the actual script to *The Conqueror* until on location and when he did he immediately became aware of the difficult dialog written for the 12th-Century warrior. By then it was too late to rewrite the entire script, but vast changes were made to ease the star's fears. Even so, Wayne failed to pull off the performance and reviewers have labeled his performance one of the worst to ever grace the screen.

Even leading lady Susan Hayward's performance has been criticized because she was insistent on looking the part of a movie star during the entire production and never a stray hair or smudge could be caught by the camera. Hayward reportedly even had one cinematographer fired from the film for shooting her with the sun shining off her nose.

Hayward herself had doubts about the role and years after being cast in the part she was quoted as saying "Me, a red-haired Tartar princess! It looked like some wild Irishman had stopped off on the road to old Cathay."

But Hughes didn't care about the miscasting. He saw Hayward as a star name to add credibility to his picture and saw the actress as a conquest of his own. The two began an affair after filming and Hayward even saw herself, for a brief time, as the future Mrs. Howard Hughes. But the affair fizzled when she became aware of his numerous other conquests.

Poor reviews have left the film to late late showings or to die-hard fans of John Wayne or its other stars. But the stars were not entirely responsible for final picture. Many aspects, from the direction to the writing, were criticized and all play some part in the final result captured on film.

Producer Hughes hired actor/director Dick Powell to direct the feature starring Wayne, Hayward, Agnes Moorehead and Pedro Armendariz. It was only Powell's second attempt at directing and the location shooting and sizable cast added to the difficult job. The budget for the RKO film was $6 million and while reports show that no major events wreaked havoc on the production, some early troubles cast a cloud over the film.

During early production much of the dialog had to be rewritten because Wayne realized he could never act his way through the difficult wording of the script. The actor's fear led him to drinking and, according to some, Wayne spent the first three days drunk, but given the difficult circumstances it seemed amazing that the star sobered up at all during the filming. The leading box office star began to question his work in the film, but continued mainly because of the money.

There were also rumors that Hayward was interested in Wayne during the production, much to the distress of his soon-to-be wife, Pilar. But no romance between the stars developed offscreen as Wayne portrayed the 12th-Century warrior and Hayward played a maid who captures his heart. Weeks of location shooting left the stars and many of the crew exposed to the elements. Dirt and sand covered much of the production crew and stars during the long days outdoors.

In addition, a flash flood narrowly missed washing the production company away early in production. And later intense heat caused problems on the set as temperatures rose as high as 120 degrees, leaving cast and crew suffering under heavy makeup and costumes.

And during filming a mishap nearly cost Pedro Armendariz his life when he was thrown from a horse when the animal stumbled. The horse then fell on top of the actor and it was initially feared the actor's back was broken, but fortunately it was not. Armendariz, however, did suffer a serious gash to his cheek and jaw requiring 26 stitches and eight days in the hospital. But mishaps and floods were only minor setbacks. The largest fear was still unknown to cast and crew and would remain so for years.

Atomic Testing

In the spring of 1953 there were numerous tests in the Nevada and Utah areas and while the reports of lambs being born dead and deformed failed to alarm anyone, Geiger counter tests by the Atomic Energy Commission (AEC) went off the roof. AEC scientists finally showed up to check for radiation. "Is it hot?" one scientist reportedly asked. "Is it hot?" came the reply. "It's so hot this needle just jumped off the pole!"

UPI

John Wayne and wife Pilar after his first battle with cancer in 1964.

Tragedy and Disaster Behind the Movies

During 1953 alone, 11 nuclear bombs were dropped within 137 miles of the film location, including one with four times the power of the bomb dropped on Hiroshima at the end of World War II. Studies say the bombings in the area accumulated fallout that is equivalent to 77 times the force of Hiroshima.

The fact that the movie location in St. George, Utah was downwind of Yucca Flat, Nevada, a common site of many bombings, meant the nuclear fallout drifted into southern Utah. And sources reported that Snow Canyon, where much location shooting was conducted, acted as a "natural reservoir" for the atomic fallout. This may have caused a delayed cancer epidemic in the state. Investigation has shown that roughly half the population of St. George developed some sort of cancer. The film crew mirrors those results.

All in all, 223 people participated in the filming. Of the cast and crew, it has been reported that at least 95 members, including Wayne, Hayward, Moorehead, Armendariz and director Powell contracted cancer-related illnesses. In addition, 300 members of the Shivwit Indian tribe were cast as extras, yet there are no figures of how many suffered the effects of the atomic testing.

Family members of the cast and crew believe today that the radiation killed their loved ones. But since many of the stars were heavy smokers, it has been reported that smoking may have caused their cancers. However, the children of Powell, Wayne and Hayward all suspected their parents were killed by atomic testing. In 1980, the children gathered at the film site to commemorate their deaths. The story was also detailed in an exhibition of photographs by Nobuho Nagasawa in 1992. The exhibit, called "The Atomic Cowboy" focuses on stars, including those in *The Conqueror*, whose deaths can be linked to atomic testing.

In an interview in 1980, Director of Radiological Health at the University of Utah, Dr. Robert Pendleton said of the high rate of cancer among cast and crew, "With these numbers, this case could qualify as an epidemic."

If the ground was a danger, the months spent on location stirring up the dirt during battle scenes and fighting didn't help as the cast and crew became covered by and inhaled the deadly dust.

And if the danger the film crew faced during the more than two months they spent on location was not enough, the director wanted to retain as much reality as possible for the studio filming that followed so he had RKO ship 60 tons of radioactive soil back to Hollywood for filming additional shots on the soundstage. This means the danger followed the cast and crew back to Hollywood and the actors spent countless more hours around the deadly earth.

Aftermath

Before the film was released Hughes sold RKO to Thomas O'Neill, the head of General Teleradio Inc. The sale came in July, 1955 with Hughes receiving $25 million for the studio, but in January of 1956 Hughes bought all rights to *The Conqueror* and another unreleased Wayne picture, *Jet Pilot*, for $8 million with an additional $4 million promised from the films' distribution profits.

The Conqueror had an advance premiere in Washington on January 24, 1956, with its national release in March. Bad reviews hurt the release and the film was forgotten quickly even though Hughes invested another $1.4 million to publicize the epic. The film grossed only $4.5 million in box office receipts, far less than the $7 million final price tag.

John Wayne died on June 11, 1979 after numerous battles with cancer. As far back as September, 1964 his battles began when cancer was discovered in his left lung. The lower part of the lung was removed along with a tumor about the size of a golf ball. Wayne survived the surgery and believed that he had won the battle.

More than a decade later, in 1978, it was discovered the actor had stomach cancer. His entire stomach and lymph nodes had to be removed in an operation that took nine and a half hours. He survived the surgery, but the cancer continued to spread and the actor underwent months of radiation treatment with little success.

In April of 1979, Wayne made his final public appearance at the Academy Awards ceremony. By May doctors found the cancer had spread throughout Wayne's body and began immunotherapy. The procedure involved injecting drugs into the body to stimulate the body's immune system to battle the cancer. It did not help. John Wayne died in June, 1979. He was 72.

Susan Hayward died in 1975 after battles with several forms of cancer. During Hayward's later years, she was diagnosed with various forms of skin cancer, breast cancer and uterine cancer. In addition, the actress was diagnosed with small tumors on her vocal cords in early 1968 and had to drop out of a Las Vegas production of *Mame*. It was only a year after having a hysterectomy to remove another growth. Then in early 1972 another tumor was discovered on one of her lungs and by 1973 more than 20 tumors were found growing at alarming rates in her brain.

During the last two years of her life the actress fought courageously as the cancerous growths destroyed her body causing terrible headaches, seizures, loss of motor skills and other physical destruction. She underwent a remission in early 1974 and agreed to appear at the Academy Awards. By the time the awards came the remission had passed and the cancer began growing again. Hayward appeared anyway, but suffered a seizure shortly after her appearance. She died less than a year later at the age of 57.

It's been reported that Hayward had heard rumors about the cast and crew of *The Conqueror* developing cancer from the atomic testing, but refused to believe the stories. Instead she continued to believe her cancer was hereditary.

Others suffered as well. Director Dick Powell died in 1963 after he contracted lymph cancer which spread to his lungs. Agnes Moorehead checked into the hospital in early April 1974 and died a month later of an "undisclosed illness." It was later reported that she died of uterine cancer at the age of 67. Not long before her death she told friend Debbie Reynolds, "I never should have taken that part." And Pedro Armendariz killed himself in 1963 at the age of 51 after reportedly learning from his doctor that he was suffering from terminal cancer of the lymph glands. Reports say he had also been battling kidney cancer.

Another actor on the movie, Jeanne Gerson, who portrayed Hayward's nurse onscreen, underwent surgery for breast and skin cancers. And even children of the stars who visited the set have since contracted forms of cancer. Patrick Wayne had a breast tumor removed in 1969. His brother Michael Wayne was treated for skin cancer in 1975. And Susan Hayward's son Tim Barker had a benign tumor removed from his mouth in 1968.

In addition to the director, other members of the crew suffered the same fate. The art director, Caroll Clark, along with a production manager and a wardrobe mistress, also died of cancer, say published reports. And the widow of Bud David, a special effects man on the film suspected the film played a role in her husband's death. Mildred David said in 1979 that her husband "suffered severe headaches" on the Utah film site and was given a medical release from the film. "He recovered and went back to work," said Mrs. David. "But for eight years he suffered from vomiting attacks. In 1971 he had an acute breathing problem, went into the hospital and died." She says the cause of death was listed as a heart attack, but he was never tested for cancer. She never linked his illness with the film until hearing the stories of other cast and crew. Published reports say as many as 55 members of the cast and crew have died of cancer.

And while the Atomic Energy Commission steadfastly denied the bombings posed a threat to the public, a federal judge in Utah awarded $2.6 million to the families of nine cancer victims in a 1980 case. Wayne's family considered a suit, but dropped the idea. One report said the family thought, "such a suit would be unpatriotic and because they didn't need the money."

Then in 1987 the government finally admitted that the Atomic Energy Commission knew of the radiation dangers, but lawyers stated the government could not be sued for damages. But, in 1988, a bill sponsored by Senator Orrin Hatch, giving partial compensation to Utah victims of cancer, was passed and some 1,100 Utah cancer victims were then eligible for compensation.

An interesting footnote to the story of *The Conqueror* is that after the film's death at the box office Howard Hughes kept the rights to the film and held it in his own private film vault. Some stories say he watched the film often in his own private theater, but refused to show it to others. It wasn't until several years after his death in 1976 and Hughes' estate was settled that the film found its way back into circulation where it eventually arrived on home video to find a new audience of Wayne fans who were not even born when the film was made.

Yet, the tragedy itself failed to stay locked away, because the whereabouts of the toxic soil shipped back to Hollywood is unknown and is still a danger. Some say the earth was disposed of locally and may have been used on Los Angeles-area playgrounds. The half-life of plutonium is 24,000 years which means the soil could be a danger for many years to come. The true horror of *The Conqueror* could continue.

Pedro Armendariz and Susan Hayward in a scene from the film.

Curse of the Silver Screen

Trog

1970

Tragedy and Disaster Behind the Movies

Crawford Cursed By *Trog*

One of Hollywood's greatest stars reaches the end of a successful career only to find a box office bomb waiting for her

It's tough surviving in the movie business. Few actors have a lifetime of work, let alone success, and even fewer can be called survivors. It easy to see the struggle by looking back at the career of Joan Crawford.

The career of Joan Crawford spanned some six decades. And even though she's no longer alive, her image has been etched in the minds of moviegoers and still finds its way to the silver screen. Whether it's a glimpse of her in an MGM rehash of *That's Entertainment,* or a photographic prop in the 1989 film *Wicked*

Stepmother, or a biopic of her life in *Mommie Dearest*, Joan Crawford lives on.

The latter all but destroyed Crawford's image, one she tried hard to protect. How much of the tell-all book by her daughter Christina is true depends on who you talk to, but Crawford was not around to defend herself or the accusations brought upon her. Her career may more be remembered by the figure displayed in the book, and by Faye Dunaway in the movie, than the one she created on the screen.

A Career Ends on a Sour Note

Crawford died of cancer at the age of 72 on May 10, 1977, but her career died approximately seven years earlier with the release of her final film, *Trog*. After a career lasting 45 years and more than 80 films, her last has been listed as her worst. Called "campy" and "deplorable," *Trog* goes down in history as one of the worst movies. It's been labeled a bomb in movie guides and TV

Joan Crawford in 'Trog.'

listings and when it's shown on late-night TV viewers are often urged to stay away.

Yet something can draw fans to the screen. Crawford's appeal had all but vanished by this point, but her fierce determination to survive kept her going. The film is worthy of viewing only for the fact that it marks her last screen appearance.

Trog was the final blow to a long an successful career. From an illustrious history as MGM's top box office draw and a string of smash hits, to her Oscar-winning performance in *Mildred*

Pierce, Joan Crawford ended up playing second fiddle to an ancient caveman. It was sad end, as *Entertainment Weekly* wrote in a 1996 feature saying that the actress is mostly remembered as the villainess in *Mommie Dearest* and "has been relegated to the dubious pantheon of camp classics, the final resting place of so many tarnished Oscar victors."

Warner Bros. released the film in 1970 and with poor reviews and a poor box office showing the film was banished to the late late show. Crawford herself refused to discuss it. She knew it was the end. It was one of the reasons she gave up performing. But her career was on the downhill by that point and there was little she could do about it. Crawford herself said in an interview with writer Roy Newquist "Now, please don't ask me about any pictures that followed *[What Ever Happened to] Baby Jane*? They were all terrible, even the few I thought might be good. I made them because I needed the money or because I was bored or both."

A New Sort of Role

The roles had grown few and far between by the early 60s when she teamed up with Bette Davis for *What Ever Happened to Baby Jane?* The film was a smash and found her a new audience. She also had a contract that gave her a nice chunk of the profits and made out better that anyone expected.

But even with the success of the film, her career was in jeopardy. The film opened up a new genre for aging actresses. Horror films were cheap to make and solid box office draw. And they kept Crawford acting. But it was a downward spiral as the movies grew worse.

Her next film, in 1963, was called *The Caretakers*, a study in mental illness that has been called inferior and did little at the box office. She exited a sequel to *Baby Jane* due to a reported illness. Although, rumors continue that it was the thought of working with Bette Davis again that made her pull out. Her next project was a horror film called *Strait-Jacket* from B-movie horror mogul William Castle.

Castle had longed to work with first-rate actors and Crawford accepted the starring role as a murderess with an ax. The film got average reviews and Crawford received a percentage of the profits along with her $50,000 salary.

Castle's next picture, *I Saw What You Did*, gave Crawford star billing even though she played fourth lead, following two teen-age girls and a killer. Crawford's character was even killed in mid-film. But Crawford was still working.

Berserk came next. Crawford's starring role in this British film about a murderer at the circus came up with enough blood and gore to draw some teens to the screen, but suffered mediocre reviews.

Berserk was the creation of producer Herman Cohen, a former movie usher who rose to fame by making low-budget horror films in England. Cut from the same cloth as William Castle, Cohen provided Crawford with star billing and a needed income. Still working as a spokesperson for Pepsi, Crawford earned no more than $50,000 a year promoting the soft drink company, which was not nearly enough to keep her living like Joan Crawford, said one biographer. Cohen, like Castle, gave Crawford two vehicles to star — *Berserk* and *Trog*.

The Story of *Trog*

Trog was written by Aben Kandel, a longtime Hollywood screenwriter who wrote a number of campy horror films including *I Was a Teenage Werewolf* and *Horrors of the Black Museum*, as well as *The Knute Rockne Story, The Iron Major* and *Dinner at Eight*. The picture was another British-made film, directed by Freddie Francis, starring Crawford as Dr. Brockton, a famous anthropologist who attempts to study an ape-like cave dweller that is half-man, half-ape, who is found by some young explorers in an underground cave. She names the beast Trog (short for Troglodyte) and tries to shape him by treating him with kindness. "We're dealing with a backward child," says Dr. Brockton. "Surely we can teach him by example." But it appears to be, and as fate would have it, the creature is incapable of being civilized and escapes.

After a brief killing spree, Trog kidnaps a young girl and hides out in a cave. Crawford manages to get Trog to release the girl before authorities use gunfire and explosives to kill Trog, putting an end to the madness. Dr. Brockton, disillusioned, wanders away from the destruction as the credits role.

Trog isn't so much a cursed production as it is a bad film. Crawford was always professional on her film sets and *Trog* was no exception, even though the film's budget was minimal and the star herself earned only about $50,000 for the leading role. There are few details about the actual production but it appears the filming was performed on schedule with filming taking place in mid-1969 and wrapping up in August of the same year. On the set, actor David Warbeck played a reporter chasing the story and recalled in a breaks between shooting Crawford giving him some words of advice. He said he was grateful for a few words she told him in the summer of 1969. "What we're paid for," she said, "is to turn shit into gold."

Crawford doesn't appear until 15 minutes into the film, but then appears in most every scene. She even manages to scale the caves, hardhat, climbing equipment and all, to find Trog along

Trog on a rampage causes destruction to a small town.

with other explorers. And at the end she ventures into the caves once again, against the advice of authorities and with absolutely no equipment. She manages to single-handedly locate the beast and the girl, reason with Trog, convincing him to let her take the girl and then climb out of the cave with the girl in her arms. Authorities then charge into the caves, now scaling its depths with extensive gear to reach the beast and then destroy it.

In some ways the film was reminiscent of *Frankenstein* with Trog as the beast and Crawford as the doctor who created/befriended it. The townspeople and authorities were out to destroy the evil monster, but the doctor wants to protect it for scientific reasons. But where *Frankenstein* succeeded, *Trog* failed. A mediocre script and limited production costs and a barely frightening caveman caused the film to be almost laughable.

Trog's producer Cohen was called an "attractive, attentive and single" producer who treated his star as exactly that — a star. He took his star to dinner and the London theater, but no romance has ever been reported. Even so, Crawford became possessive. She would call him late at night to talk over the script and would demand to know where he was when he wasn't there to take her calls.

It was fairly public knowledge that Crawford drank while working during her last years. Often it was disguised by her mixing vodka with a bottle of Pepsi Cola, but many knew. She promoted the soft drink in the late 50s when her last husband, Alfred Steele, was a top executive with the cola company. Crawford brought coolers of it to her movie sets and even managed to have it displayed onscreen throughout several of her later films. Everyone knew she added something to her Pepsi. But even so, Crawford never had trouble remembering her lines or cause a delay in production.

Image of a Movie Star

Crawford, forever the professional, even had to change costumes in a car during location shooting because the low budget production didn't supply portable dressing rooms.

The star supplied her own clothes for wardrobe on her last few films, telling Cohen to save his money for other production costs. And when it came time to begin location shooting she arrived on the set in the gray English moors with 38 pieces of luggage.

There were also rumors the star had a face lift before the film, but they were not true. On *Berserk* and *Trog* she enjoyed the services of a gifted hairstylist named Ramon Guy who had performed his magic on another aging actress — Marlene Dietrich.

For her final films, stylist Guy devised a series of six "lifts." These "lifts" were small tapes connected to rubber bands that came together behind the head and lifted and stretched the skin — erasing wrinkles and years.

She also had another beauty tip, which she once told to a woman's magazine writer. "There's a trick, Claudette Colbert taught me years ago. Dump a tray of ice in your wash basin and splash ice water on your bazooms. It keeps them firm."

But beauty tips didn't erase the poor production and the bad reviews that followed.

A Forgettable Release

Crawford herself summed up *Trog* and her other flops by saying "At least a dozen of my bad pictures would have been good ones had they been given a decent script and a strong director."

Joan Crawford in later years.

Tragedy and Disaster Behind the Movies

The New York Times reviewed the film after its release in October, 1970. Writer A.H. Weiler wrote *Trog* "proves that Joan Crawford is grimly working at her craft. Unfortunately, the determined lady, who is fetching in a variety of chic pant suits and dresses, has little else going for her. ... *Trog* is no more exciting or scientific than the antics of a rambunctious kid in a progressive school."

In the end, the film received little notice and few film historians and Crawford biographers even discuss the film in regards to Crawford's career. Some say that *Trog* had "little significance" on the star's career and that it was only because of the star's status that the movie wasn't tossed into the "B" movie category.

Crawford retired shortly after the film's release, filming an occasional guest appearance on television or making a rare public appearance and tried to forget the making of *Trog*. She was rarely seen in public after her retirement. Dore Freeman, a longtime fan and collector of Crawford memorabilia, told the *New York Times* in 1977 that she all but vanished from public view. His autograph collection and correspondence with Crawford spanned 40 years. His last autograph from her came in October 1971, about a year after *Trog*'s release. "During the last years she never liked to go out into public anymore," he said. "She was a movie star, a glamour queen. It would take so much time to prepare herself to be seen. Why do it? Nobody gave her any jobs."

When she died in May 1977, obituaries and features reflecting on her career detailed a rich and successful body of work of critically-acclaimed films, box office hits and a superstar image that made her famous. Few discussed, or even mentioned, her final film — *Trog*. She probably would have been grateful.

One interesting footnote to the career of Joan Crawford was that in 1977 the producers of the multi-million dollar movie adventure *Superman* had felt they had made a casting coup when they decided that no one would be a better mother for Superman than Joan Crawford when they cast her in the role of Ma Kent, opposite Glen Ford's Pa Kent. But the renaissance would never take place because no sooner had the producers put in a call to Crawford's agent to offer her the part when they heard on the radio that the star had died. The part went to the producer's mother in law and Joan Crawford's return to the big screen was never realized.

Tragedy and Disaster Behind the Movies

Curse of the Silver Screen

The Exorcist

1973

Tragedy and Disaster Behind the Movies

Terror of 'The Exorcist' — On & Off the Screen

A true horror story leads to a series of troubled big screen features

In 1949 the story of a young boy possessed by demons made headlines in the *Washington Post,* becoming one of the most widely publicized cases of demonic possession in the 20th century.

Reports said a 14-year-old boy living on Bunker Hill Road in Mt. Rainier, Maryland, was suspected of being demonically possessed when his parents began to notice bizarre occurrences like scratching sounds beneath his bed, furniture sliding across his bedroom floor, levitation of objects around him and red welts appearing on his body. The parents took the boy to several doctors, but no medical explanation could be found. The parents eventually turned to a local priest who diagnosed the situation as a case of possession and requested permission from the church to perform an exorcism.

Over a two-month period Reverend Albert Hughes reportedly carried out nearly 30 rights of exorcism, during which time the boy responded with anger, lashing out at Rev. Hughes and his parents by cursing, kicking and fighting anyone who came near. It was even said the boy spoke in Latin, although he had no knowledge of the language. When the boy was forced to wear a crucifix he became even more violent and as many as five additional priests were called in to restrain the youth. The story goes that finally the demon announced itself, speaking through the boy, and then quickly departed. Once gone, the boy had no recollection of what had transpired. The story was logged into the official Roman archives by Rev. Hughes as an actual case of demonic possession and faded into history.

Extraordinary Story Leads to Book

While a student at Georgetown University, William Peter Blatty read of the case and used it as the basis of a novel which he called, appropriately enough, *The Exorcist*. During the writing of the book, Blatty said he began experimenting with a Ouija board one morning and found himself caught up in an extraordinary dialogue with the dead. "I [started] at 9 in the morning. I was still there at 10 a.m. the next day," noted Blatty, who claims to have contacted his deceased father and a teenage girl who lived during the 15th century in central Europe.

The book became a best seller in 1971, eventually selling six million copies, and was translated into 18 different languages. Blatty was also awarded a Silver Medal for Literature from the

Commonwealth Club of California for his work.

Soon there was talk of turning it into a film. But turning the book into a filmable feature became a daunting task that Blatty himself took on. In the first draft of the screenplay he reportedly toned down much of the graphic violence and profanity because he felt the motion picture rating board would never allow the film to be shown without carrying the dreaded X rating.

When William Friedkin, the director hired to make the film, saw the first screenplay he urged Blatty to produce another draft that more closely resembled the book. The screenplay that came forth satisfied both writer and director and pre-production kicked into high gear. Friedkin actually wasn't the first choice for direction. A list of several well-known directors, including Stanley Kubrick, Mike Nichols and Arthur Penn, was considered first. Blatty himself suggested Friedkin after having met him several years before, and when the other directors were unavailable or turned the project down, Friedkin became the obvious choice.

Unlike the story it was based, both the book and the screenplay featured a young girl as the possessed child. For casting of the key role as many as 500 young girls were considered before a 14-year-old Linda Blair was chosen for the part of Regan MacNeil. Blair began her career at the age of five, modeling in catalogues for Sears and Macy's, among others. When she was six she was performing in commercials for fabric softener, grape jelly and cereal. Steady work and an extensive resume brought her to the attention of the producers. But Friedkin met with Blair as many as 15 times before he was convinced she was right for the role.

In addition to Blair, the role of Regan's mother Chris was integral to the story. Several actresses were considered and even offered the part, including Jane Fonda and Shirley MacLaine. MacLaine actually served as a model for the character because she was a neighbor and friend of Blatty's and he crafted the part with her in mind, but when the terms of the deal could not be ironed out Ellen Burstyn was cast in the role. Other featured stars included actor Max von Sydow who was chosen as Father Merrin, Jason Miller as Father Karras, Lee J. Cobb was selected for the part of Lt. Kinderman, and Jack MacGowran took the role of Burke

Dennings. Once the remaining cast and crew were selected filming began.

Filming Takes Longer Than Normal

Location filming took place mainly in Georgetown with some footage captured in New York and some of the early scenes of the film were captured with footage shot in Flagstaff, Arizona and in an area near Baghdad, Iraq. The budget was originally set at about $4 million, but production expenses stretched far beyond the original plan. While the average film takes roughly three months to shoot, filming on *The Exorcist*, took some 180 days and the final cost was pegged at $10 million. Production problems plagued the movie to the point that some began to fear the film itself was demonically possessed.

During production a carpenter lost several fingers in a construction mishap, a mysterious fire destroyed a film stage and there were even rumors that some of the film reels used in production came up blank after they were processed. Blatty made himself present for the entire filming to ensure the feature kept with the story he created, and after the eerie events and mishaps became all too commonplace, Blatty took matters into his own hands and asked a priest from his Catholic high school to come in an bless the set.

Death was a key part of the script for several characters. For Jack MacGowran, it wasn't only written in the script. MacGowran himself met an untimely end not long after the death of his character.

The Exorcist's character of Burke Dennings was a director and friend to Regan's mother Chris, who was an actress making a film in the Georgetown area. After Regan is taken over by a demon, Dennings is asked to watch the young girl for a short time when Chris' assistant leaves the house to get the girl some medication. When Chris returns home and finds no one in the house watching Regan she responds angrily to her assistant who has just returned. The assistant says she had asked Dennings to watch the girl. A moment later a knock at the door brings news that Dennings fell to his death down a stairway outside the house.

Police initially suspect he was drunk and fell down the stairs, but circumstances later lead them to believe he was killed and thrown from the window. It turns out that the demon threw Dennings to his death from Regan's bedroom window.

MacGowran finished filming his portion of *The Exorcist* in the third week of December and, once his character was dead, he stayed on in New York to appear in a play called *The Plough and the Stars*, which he had been rehearsing during his off hours of filming. But earlier in the month he felt a sharp pain in his chest while walking down the street on a cold December day and a doctor in Long Island diagnosed the problem as a heart condition in which the arteries become hardened and are unable to deliver the required amount of oxygen to the heart. McGowran was ordered to rest.

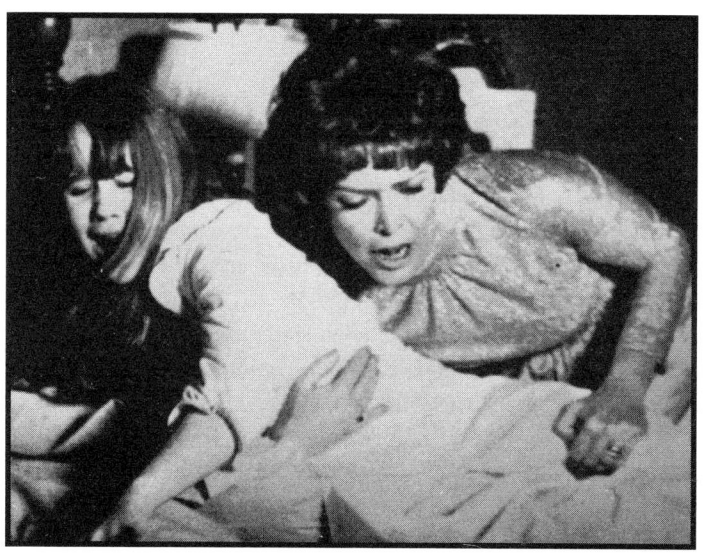

Linda Blair and Ellen Burstyn in a scene from the film.

The actor did get some extra rest, but was still juggling his film and theater work. When his film production wrapped he directed his efforts to the play, but on Friday, January 26 he was hit with the flu and ended up in bed. He was staying at the Algonquin Hotel and spent the weekend resting. On Monday he claimed he felt well enough to return to work, but he quickly became too weak and pale. That evening, while resting he bed, he was talking with a friend when he suddenly said, "I feel very tired, Darling," and he took a deep breath. He then put his head back on his pillow, closed his eyes and died. He was 54. It took the cast and crew by surprise.

A Plethora of Special Effects

Production on *The Exorcist* continued. Some of the difficulties came from the special effects work involving Blair during the latter part of the film where demons have taken over her body. The exorcism scenes took roughly three months to film because Friedkin wanted a particular feel to the climactic final portion of the film — cold.

The director wanted Regan's bedroom to become unbelievably cold as the possession progressed. To get the correct feel the bedroom was constructed on a refrigerated set of a large studio soundstage. Air conditioners were run each night to get the temperature down as far as 40 degrees below zero, some claim. Once the actors and crew took their places, and the lights and equipment were up and running, the temperature would rise above the zero mark, but the set would remain cold enough for the actors' breath to be visible on film, which was the effect that Friedkin was after. But the actors, crew and equipment found filming in the frigid cold difficult and there were numerous days when not a single shot was captured on film.

Make-up artist Dick Smith has been credited for providing much of the visual impact through his work of turning young Linda Blair into the demon child necessary to scare viewers. One particularly challenging scene in the script called for the words "help me" to rise through Regan's skin just below her rib cage. To accomplish the scene Smith used a substance that would disappear and painted the words on Blair's skin. The words appeared on her body for a moment and then faded away. The scene was filmed and for the final print the footage was run backward so it would appear as if the words appeared instead of disappeared.

Curse of the Silver Screen

Blockbuster Impacted by Real Horror

The Exorcist was released in late 1973 in time for Academy Award consideration. It was an immediate hit. The film became one of the most successful motion pictures in history grossing more than $165 million in its domestic release. It became the fifth highest grossing film of the 1970s and Warner Bros. biggest money-maker to date and became the highest grossing horror film ever according to *Variety*. But it was certainly not without controversy.

Moviegoers fainted, vomited and some were so scared they went running from the theaters. Many were outraged by the violent nature of the film and urged viewers to stay away. Some countries banned the film from being shown while some cities in the U.S. barred children from seeing the film. And the Roman Catholic church reported an unusually high number of people requesting that clergy perform rights of exorcism because they believed they were possessed after seeing the horror film.

At least one moviegoer took things to an extreme. James Schoenfeld became obsessed with the film, writing in his diary in 1975, "I must learn how to insure myself from becoming possessed." During the time he saw the film, Schoenfeld was in the planning stages of a horrendous crime and the effect the film had on him may have played a role in the events that transpired. "If I make it through the night, it will be a miracle," he wrote after returning from the screening. "This movie is already playing tricks on me."

At gunpoint, Schoenfeld, along with his brother Richard and another man, Fred Woods, kidnapped 26 schoolchildren and a bus driver on a bus in July, 1976 and ordered them into a poorly ventilated moving van which the trio then buried in a quarry near Livermore, a town in San Joaquin Valley, California. The kidnappers then demanded a $5 million ransom from authorities before they released the children. The school children and their driver were buried for more than 16 hours before managing to dig themselves free and go for help. The kidnappers were later arrested, tried and sentenced to life in prison.

In its initial release *The Exorcist* was greeted with

excellent reviews and an amazing box office popularity. When the Academy Awards announced the nominees for 1973 the film was honored with several nominations, including Best Director for Friedkin and Best Actress for Burstyn. But it was Blatty who walked off with the Oscar for Best Screenplay. The only other Academy Award the film captured that year was for sound editing.

After the immense success, everyone wanted their share of the fame and fortune. For the voice of the devil, actress Mercedes McCambridge was used for the vocals of Regan as the devil. McCambridge, who is best known for her starring roles in *Giant* and *Johnny Guitar,* sued Warner Bros. because she was not credited for her contribution to the film. In addition, both Blatty and Friedkin filed separate suits against the studio claiming they had not received their fair share of the profits from the box office success.

A Sequel On the Horizon

Even with legal troubles and the numerous reports of attempted exorcisms, and people claiming possession by the devil, Warner Bros. set its sights on a sequel. *Exorcist II — The Heretic* followed in 1977 hoping to recapture the success of the original. Neither Blatty nor Friedkin took part in the creation of the second film and actress Ellen Burstyn turned down an offer to star in the feature. Linda Blair, however, agreed to take part, but the film was a tremendous failure and Blair's career has been plagued by typecasting ever since.

Lee J. Cobb and Jason Miller

If the original film was the blockbuster of horror films, then its sequel was the ultimate bomb. With an $11 million budget, the long-awaited film starred Richard Burton and Louise Fletcher along with Blair following the life of Regan several years after the original story ended.

When it came to the release pre-publicity created strong interest and exhibitors were asked to put up excessive sums of money to secure a chance to show the picture. Usually, exhibitors get a chance to view some or all of a film before they invest, but in the case of *Exorcist II*, theater owners put up as much as $150,000 for the opportunity to show the film with only Hollywood promises of a blockbuster to go on.

Opening week appeared promising with the movie grossing almost $925,000 in June 1977, but dismal reviews and poor word of mouth spelled disaster when profits dropped to roughly $430,000 in its second week of release. One reviewer said "There is a very strong probability that *Exorcist II* is the stupidest major movie ever made."

Director John Boorman was asked to step back into the editing room and try and save the picture. In a rush effort, with the movie already playing in movie houses across the country, Boorman phoned in about three minutes in cuts to the film from his home in Ireland. The new version was rushed to more than 700 theaters at once. Boorman then began an even more drastic reworking of the film, eliminating about 20 minutes of the feature, much of which included Richard Burton, and added 10 new minutes of footage. The next version was used in the film's foreign release, but even with the reworking the sequel was labeled a box office failure.

Final Film Makes it a Trilogy

Then in 1983, William Blatty wrote a novel called *Legion* which detailed the story of William Kinderman, a detective that was part of the original film, who this time is investigating a series of ritualistic murders. Blatty decided the book would serve as a suitable feature to continue *The Exorcist* series and developed the book into a screenplay which he himself would direct. In order to craft the story into a suitable member of the series, Blatty had to add the theme of possession and an exorcism to the screenplay since neither were a part of the book from which the story was based.

Other than Kinderman, none of the original characters returned for *The Exorcist: 1990*, but the setting of Georgetown once again was used as a backdrop. George C. Scott was cast in the lead role, originally played by Lee J. Cobb.

But again the film failed to capture the thrill of the original. This time, to avoid the disaster of the first sequel, test audiences were used to predict the success at the box office. When preview audiences didn't respond positively to the feature Blatty rewrote and reshot $9 million worth of film. And minimal pre-publicity was used to open the film, hoping word of mouth would help the picture.

In its first week the film brought in $9.3 million, making it the number one movie at the box office. *The Exorcist* name helped draw early crowds, but word of mouth didn't help the feature, which quickly faded from the box office, faring slightly better that the second sequel. The series came to a close, but the curse of *The Exorcist* didn't end with the big screen.

A Neighborhood Cursed

For the neighbors that live on Bunker Hill Road in Mount Rainier the opportunity to have their neighborhood featured onscreen for the filming of *The Exorcist* was probably a highlight of 1972 and 1973. The lasting success of the horror classic continues to be a reminder of that time as well, but a series of tragedies has also plagued the neighborhood where the young boy who inspired the film underwent an exorcism in 1949.

The house where the little boy lived came down in the mid 1960s when it was destroyed by fire during a training exercise by the Mount Rainier volunteer fire department.

After the filming, the staircase near the house became a popular stop for tourists. And in 1982, a strange series of tragic events began to trouble those who lived nearby.

In a bar in March 1982, Ellen Day told Robert Hoffman, her common-law husband, that she was having an affair. Hoffman went home and called his sister, telling her he was going to kill Day when she came home and true to his word, when the woman returned home the next morning, Hoffman shot her to death with his hunting rifle inside their Bunker Hill Road home. He was later sentenced to 30 years in prison.

In April 1983, little more than a year later, a house on the corner caught fire trapping 68-year-old Della Weakley inside. Her cause of death was listed as accidental, but investigators suspected that smoking may have led to the blaze.

Then, in the summer of the same year, John Planer, a 20-year-old man was stabbed to death in Ocean City, Maryland while staying at a friend's house. The friend's brother, Ricky Peter Clark reportedly awoke in the night, killed Planer with no explanation taking his body to a nearby creek where he tied the body down with concrete blocks and dumped it in the water. Clark was later found guilty of first-degree murder, but not responsible by reason of insanity and was institutionalized. Planer and his family lived on Bunker Hill Road.

In June, 1984 another fire ripped through a brick townhouse in the neighborhood killing 28-year-old Scott Woodcock. That same week, Danny Velasquez, a neighbor who lived across the street from Woodcock, suddenly slipped into a coma, dying two weeks later. Diabetes was suspected as a cause of his death.

Then in May 1985, violence struck again on Bunker Hill Road when Francois Robert Bourgeau was charged with the murders of Darrenna Shelton and her sister when she failed to pay her rent. Bourgeau went to the building he owned, where Shelton, who was his tenant, was living. He shot both women to death and torched the building which he owned.

Since then the eerie stories of the cursed neighborhood have continued the tale of the curse of *The Exorcist*. Both the real and the filmed versions continue to thrive promising that the fascinating story behind the movie will live for many years to come.

Tragedy and Disaster Behind the Movies

Superman

1978

Tragedy and Disaster Behind the Movies

Stars of Superman Suffer Tragedy

A Trio of Actors Make It Through a Difficult Filming Only to be Linked by a Series of Personal Tragedies

The comic book hero Superman was a natural for the big screen. From movie serials in the 40s to television in the 50s, the man of steel captured the imaginations of several generations. And like most great ideas in the entertainment world, which find themselves brought back to life every few decades, the idea was due for a return and the timing was perfect.

Space-age epics like *Star Wars* set the stage for bigger and better, and *Superman* fit the bill. *Star Wars* cost a mere $10.5 million and grossed a whopping $185.1 million in its initial release. The producers of *Superman* hoped they could do the same with a larger-than-life Man of Steel.. And while *Superman* went on to become one of the blockbusters of the 1970s, the expense and production troubles went way beyond *Star Wars*. And looking back years later it appears the stars of *Superman* are linked again by a bizarre series of tragedies that forever changed their lives.

An Idea Reborn

Producers Alexander Salkind, his son Ilya, and Pierre Spengler were independent filmmakers who first caught the attention of Hollywood in 1973 with their feature *The Three Musketeers*. It wasn't that the movie was a blockbuster, or that it was a critically-acclaimed masterpiece. What made the film remarkable was that it became two films. The producers found themselves with so much extra footage at the end of *The Three Musketeers* that they simply cut the film in half, did some editing and created *The Four Musketeers*. Two films at the cost of only one proved to be both ingenious and profitable. And in the fall of 1973, the idea of filming two features of *Superman* at once seemed too good to be true. And this time it was.

Christopher Reeve and Margot Kidder in 'Superman.'

Ilya Salkind had an idea of an epic production of *Superman*. His father liked the idea, as did Spengler. Once the financiers were in line the trio set off to make their movie — or movies.

By late 1974 the producers had convinced Warner

Communications, owners of National Periodical Publications, the company that owned the Superman character, that they would maintain the integrity of the Man of Steel. And once this was done they set forth on creating a script and hoped to begin filming in 1975.

Mario Puzo, of *The Godfather* fame, was hired to create the script. A draft came forth in April and production was initially set to begin in November 1975. A second draft arrived in October, but due to its extensive length, the producers needed help cutting it down. Puzo was already committed to other projects by this time and suggested the producers find someone else to do the work. Robert Benton and David and Leslie Newman, the team that gave *Bonnie and Clyde* life, were brought in to do the job.

Next it was time to find a director. Steven Spielberg's name came up first and the producers knew his latest movie was about to come out. They decided to wait and see how it looked. It was *Jaws* and it was a blockbuster. But by then it was too late and Spielberg was already signed to direct several features as part of a multi-picture deal.

William Freidkin (*The Exorcist*), Francis Ford Coppola (*Apocalypse Now*), John Guillermin (*The Towering Inferno*), Robert Aldrich (*What Ever Happened to Baby Jane?*) and every other major Hollywood director was approached, but all were tied to other projects.

Another director, Guy Hamilton, accepted then dropped out when finally Richard Donner, who found success with *The Omen*, was brought on board and began planning the movie he was about to direct.

Production, first set for Rome, was now shifted to London, and before the producers realized it, 1976 had come and gone and casting was finally ready to begin in early 1977.

To get a major star on board would give the big budget feature a name behind it and support the financiers would feel comfortable with and the media and public would take notice of. Marlon Brando was that name. Brando was signed to the role of Jor-El, Superman's father, in the summer of 1976 while an extensive search went on for the appropriate Superman. Brando's salary, for 13 days of shooting, was an amazing $3.7 million and set the stage for the record-breaking salaries of years to come. Total budget for the production was expected to be $40 million.

For the role of the Man of Steel the search actually began in early 1975 and by late 1976 the producers still had not found their star. Everyone was considered and many were approached, but no Superman was found. Paul Newman, Robert Redford, Ryan O'Neal, Clint Eastwood, Steve McQueen, Bruce Jenner, Nick Nolte, Burt Reynolds, John Beck, Perry King, Jeff Bridges, David Soul, Robert Wagner, Kris Kristofferson and countless others were considered. Some turned down the role, some were unavailable, some were only considered.

Finally, by mid-1977, Christopher Reeve was found and hired to play Superman. His salary was a mere $250,000. Initially producers weren't sure he had the look, but deciding that he could become the superhero with the proper makeup and some added muscle, the decision was made.

For the role of Lois Lane, a similar search went on with Margot Kidder finally landing the role. Others considered included Natalie Wood, Carrie Fisher, Shirley MacLaine, Christina Raines, Liza Minelli, Jill Clayburg, Leslie Ann Warren, Jessica Lange and even Barbra Steisand.

The other cast members included Ned Beatty, Valerie Perrine, Marc McClure and Susanna York. And Gene Hackman was signed to the role of evil Lex Luthor for $2 million. An established crew, many of whom helped bring *Star Wars* to life, was also assembled.

Production Begins At Last

Production finally began on March 28, 1977 at Shepperton Studios in England. Filming was expected to carry cast and crew from England to the United States, Canada, South America, Australia and a number of other countries. Production problems and a skyrocketing budget plagued the filming from the start and many plans were nixed, altered or changed. Problems on the set ranged from general production mishaps, to actors dropping out at the last minute, to death.

One key dilemma was in making Superman fly. Several

different methods were used. One standard method had Reeve suspended by wires, but on film the wires showed and the shots had to be redone. Another flying shot called for a panoramic skyline which took a substantial portion of the set. Several curved screens were used to get the wide shot, but on film the areas where the screens were joined together showed and the scene, again, had to be reshot. A team was put together to test a variety of harnesses, hydraulic armatures, cranes, animated models, weightless chambers and more to make Superman's time in the air look real. Loads of options were tested and in the end hundreds of flying shots were filmed, while only the few methods that worked found their way onto the screen.

Brando's 13-days of filming went by quickly with minor delays and production problems due to the destruction of the planet Krypton. Massive sets were blown up, but getting the debris to fall on cue with the actors fleeing took time and effort to make the scenes look real. In one scene, a camera lense burst from intense heat sending shards glass across the set. Fortunately no one was hurt. Near the end of his time on the set, Brando was asked what he thought about playing the role of Superman's father. "I think I'll make a lot of money," was the actor's reply.

Marlon Brando

Superman Can't Sweat

Another problem during filming again involved Reeve. No one planned for the superhero to sweat under the hot lights during shooting and Reeve's perspiration showed through on the costume. Special pads had to be designed to fit the costume to hide the perspiration and make Superman's efforts look easy.

By May, the filming was already a week behind in production. Division between the director and producers developed as the production gap continued to widen. The director wanted a first-class picture and refused to compromise the filming in order to keep it on schedule. The producers also wanted a first-rate film, but concerns about the exploding budget and inability to finish on time frustrated them.

By June the filming was two weeks behind schedule. To make up time, location shooting on *Superman II* was put on hold and all efforts were concentrated on the first feature, although soundstage filming of the sequel did continue to utilize the availability of the actors.

Filming had expanded to two studios by June and scenes involving Clark Kent and the *Daily Planet* were ready to begin when a new problem arose. The newsroom sets were constructed at Pinewood Studios, but the role of newspaper editor Perry White had not been cast. Finally, at the last minute, Jack Klugman was cast in the role after the producers had considered numerous actors including Martin Balsam, Walter Matthau, Jason Robards and Ed Asner.

Filming was to begin on Wednesday and the decision was made on Monday with Klugman expected at the studios on Tuesday. But as arrangements were being finalized and costume designers were busy tailoring clothes to fit the star, Klugman's agent phoned to say the actor had turned down the part. A "backup" choice, Eddie Albert was assigned the part and costume designers frantically shifted gears. When Albert's agent phoned to say the actor would take the part only after renegotiating the salary, the producers looked for another option. Keenan Wynn was quickly selected and flew to London. He was rushed through fittings, make-up and lighting tests because the crew had already spent two days filming around his character. But before he could step before the cameras Wynn was rushed to the hospital with chest pains. Suffering from "extreme exhaustion," the actor had to bow out of the role. Finally, Jackie Cooper was approached and agreed to take over the role and filming with Perry White finally took place.

Problems continued throughout the *Daily Planet* shooting when the power to the studio blew out due to the extensive lighting of the newsroom scenes. Then, because of the intense heat from the lighting, the studio's sprinkler system went off, drenching the set in water. Shooting was now three weeks behind schedule. Talks between the director and the producers grew angrier as threats of legal action were tossed into the mix. Producers began to fear that the director's slow pace was costing the production millions and the director claimed the producers were trying to make cutbacks that threatened his ability to make a successful picture.

Superman Soars to New York

Rumors hit Hollywood that Donner would be replaced as director by Richard Lester, whom the producers had worked with on *The Three Musketeers*. Lester was brought in, but he was brought in only as an advisor and Donner continued directing. The set was divided in support of Donner and support for the producers. Tension was ripe when the production took off for the United States and shooting in New York City.

Kidder, as Lois Lane, shares a kiss with Reeve's Superman.

But a new location didn't help matters and production troubles were only magnified. The building for New York newspaper the *Daily News* was used as the *Daily Planet* offices for exterior shooting and each night it cost $2,000 to have the exact lighting of the offices replicated. Production notes also say that similar lighting situations for shooting on Wall Street cost $7,500 a night.

On July 13, filming was set to begin as usual when a blackout hit New York and production came to an abrupt halt. It was feared that the intense lighting of the *Daily News* building and the additional production lights caused the blackout, but it turned out to be an electrical storm. Fortunately, insurance covered the cost of the delay, but figures for the New York shooting reached nearly $3 million when it was initially pegged at costing only about $500,000.

Filming next moved to Canada and British Columbia, where bad weather dogged the crew, delaying needed exterior shots including a train sequence in which the filmmakers rented a train for $5,000 a day. Weather forecasts continued to predict bad weather and by late August location shooting finally wrapped and the crew returned to London only to find much of what was filmed was useless. It was decided that *Superman II* would have to wait while the crew concentrated all efforts on finishing *Superman*.

Production Woes Continue

Production inside the studio had crew members asking for what was referred to as "hardship pay" from the difficult and long shooting schedules. The crew even threatened to walk out, but the problems were eventually worked out and filming continued.

By the fall, principal photography took a break until late November. When cast and crew returned they found that now it was a lack of funds that had cast a cloud over the future of the film. Filming continued however when Donner met with the top brass at Warner Bros. and convinced them the film had to be completed under his vision, even with the delays.

But when 1978 arrived things only got worse. A stunt man took a serious fall during a flying scene, falling 40 feet to the ground. Fortunately, he escaped serious injury, but on the same day another crew member wasn't as lucky. Reports say that a metal worker was crushed to death when a replica of Air Force One, which was built for a key scene in the film, collapsed on top of him.

Within a week it was announced that *Superman* would not make its planned arrival of April 15, 1978 and the release was pushed back until December. Cast and crew breathed a sigh of relief once the initial shock of the announcement wore off knowing the change bought them more time.

Even so, by March things didn't look much better for finishing *Superman* and the director began the task of eliminating any filming that wasn't absolutely necessary to completing the picture. Location shooting in Finland was canceled and some inferior footage that Donner had hoped to reshoot was left in. One additional desert scene was filmed on location in New Mexico, but more delays followed in April when bad weather kept the crew from filming a scene for 15 days. It was a crucial scene where a dam breaks and Superman heads to the rescue. Filming continued through the summer, finally wrapping in August.

The Film is Finally Finished

In the end, more than 1,000 people took part in making the film and 1,250,000 feet of film was shot. *Superman* was complete, but its sequel *Superman II* was not and would need additional production work and more money before it could be finished. The original film took a total of 350 days of shooting and the film went several million dollars over budget. Editing and special optical effects then became the most important job. But finally *Superman* was finished and ready for theaters.

Promotional trailers for the film began running in early 1978 and by December the public was ready to see the finished project. It was a sure crowd pleaser and fans and reviewers received the film warmly.

While the reported cost was listed at $40 million it's important to note that *Superman II,* which was largely filmed in conjunction with *Superman* also cost $40 million to produce. And while it was initially intended that both films could be made at the same time under roughly one budget, in the final view the producers found it nearly impossible to complete the first film, let alone its successor. The gross receipts came in at more than $82.5 million, ranking the movie as Warner Bros. second most successful venture for the decade, behind only *The Exorcist*. It was the seventh most successful film of the decade of all pictures released.

The success of the first ensured the completion of the sequel and led to two more features. By the time *Superman III* and *Superman IV* were made production wrinkles had been ironed out. And while the features were not as costly, they also were not as profitable, but enough so to continue drawing moviegoers. In 1987, the final film of the series *Superman IV — The Quest for Peace,* was released.

Trouble Follows the Stars

But the *Superman* saga continued when a series of bizarre tragedies befell the three leading stars of the troubled film. Marlon Brando, Margot Kidder and Christopher Reeve have each suffered devastating losses that have changed their lives forever.

In 1989, Brando's daughter Cheyenne suffered a near fatal car crash in Tahiti after a rumored argument with her father. Brando had his daughter flown to Los Angeles where he stayed at her bedside and spent millions of dollars on plastic surgery to repair the damage to her face.

During her recovery she became involved with Dag Drollet, a six-foot-five Tahitian. Cheyenne became pregnant and it was May, 1990 when Cheyenne, who was seven months pregnant, told her half-brother Christian that her boyfriend, Drollet, had beaten her. In his anger Christian Brando shot Drollet to death with a .45 caliber handgun during a struggle inside Marlon Brando's Los Angeles mansion. The younger Brando was charged with murder in July, 1990 and pleaded guilty to voluntary manslaughter in early 1991. His father put up his $4 million estate as collateral to secure bail, but the younger Brando was later sentenced to 10 years in prison. During the trial Marlon Brando broke a long public silence, telling reporters he became recluse to maintain his sanity. "This [Hollywood] is a false world," said Brando. "and it's been a struggle to preserve your sanity in a world that has been taken away from you."

Charges against his daughter for complicity in the murder were dropped in 1993 when her lawyer pleaded that the legal proceedings had caused his client to suffer from severe depression that endangered her life. Even with the charges dropped Cheyenne continued to battle depression and tried to commit suicide three times. The final time, in April, 1995 Cheyenne Brando successfully hanged herself in the bedroom of her home in Tahiti. Marlon Brando was devastated by the tragedy and was reportedly hospitalized. He declined to comment and has rarely spoken to the press of the troubles that have plagued his family.

Margot's Breakdown

For Margot Kidder trouble began in late 1990 when she was involved in a car accident during the filming of a television series based on the Nancy Drew books. Kidder, who was driving the car with actress Polly Bergen as the passenger, claimed the brakes locked and she and Bergen were thrown forward. Kidder sued the producers of the series believing she had suffered permanent injuries which caused her muscle spasms in her neck and back, in addition to numbness and lack of circulation in her left leg. She also said she suffered nerve damage to her left arm, shoulder and her neck. And due to her inability to work, Kidder claimed she was fired by the producers.

It was later discovered that Kidder was also afflicted with a manic-depressive disorder. And in April, 1996 she disappeared for several days. She was finally found in the backyard of a home in Glendale, CA holding a knife and looking disheveled, claiming someone was trying to kill her. Her hair appeared to have been chopped off, she had lost her dentures and said she had been wandering Los Angeles. She said that two homeless men attempted to comfort her, but later tried to rape her. She was taken to a psychiatric ward at Olive Medical Center and placed under observation.

The story of her breakdown made newspapers and television news shows across the country and to recover Kidder retreated to a cabin in Montana. She has since made a full recovery, returning to acting and speaking candidly about her bouts with mental illness.

Superman's Tragic Fall

Superman himself met with tragedy on May 27, 1995 when Christopher Reeve was thrown from a horse during trials of an equestrian event in Virginia. Reeve, who has been called an expert equestrian, was competing in a dressage competition when the seven-year old roan gelding he was riding came to an abrupt halt as it approached the third of 15 jumps. The actor was wearing both a riding helmet and a safety vest at the time, but Reeve hit the ground head first, breaking his neck. The accident left him paralyzed and unable to breath. It was initially feared he had severed his spinal cord, but doctors later confirmed that was not the case, leaving Reeve with the hope he may walk again.

The actor spent months recovering, developed pneumonia and underwent a delicate six-hour operation to repair injuries to his vertebrae. Intense therapy has enabled Reeve to breathe on his own, sit up, speak and become a spokesperson for the disabled while focusing the media's attention on spinal injuries and medical efforts to cure many of those afflicted. Reeve is convinced he will walk again. Ironically enough, the actor's last role before the accident was in the HBO film *Above Suspicion* in which he starred as a police detective who is confined to a wheel chair after his spine was severed by a bullet.

Superman takes Lois Lane for a ride.

Conclusion

It's impossible to predict what might have been had the movies chronicled here never been made. But the fascinating possibilities are endless.

What might have come of those surrounding *Rosemary's Baby* if the film had never been produced. Would William Castle's career have continued in low-grade pictures? And what of Roman Polanski? Would his wife, Sharon Tate been murdered that night in Benedict Canyon or would they never have moved into the house Charles Manson's followers broke into in 1969? It's a bit of a stretch to suspect that Manson would not have taken his "family" on a killing spree that year, unless, that is, one truly believes in a curse on *Rosemary's Baby.*

And what of *The Misfits*? Would Clark Gable have lived to see the birth of his son and gone on to make more classic motion pictures? It's impossible to say, but suspicion that the strain of the movie on his health leads one to believe that he may very well have. Marilyn Monroe's marriage might not have suffered the strain it did through the making of the film and her marriage to Arthur Miller might have lasted through that summer in 1962 when she died of an overdose.

The trouble with *The Exorcist* started long before the film, but the film's influence on others changed numerous lives. And Joan Crawford's career could have survived and undergone a renaissance with one strong role that might have kept her performing had she not starred in *Trog*. And *Superman* would not have helped set the stage for massive celebrity salaries and exploding budgets to capture box office dollars.

Rebel Without a Cause is certainly a classic and it's impossible to imagine the careers of its three stars had the movie never made it to the big screen. James Dean's legend would certainly be different, but possibly not. Who knows the paths that Natalie Wood and Sal Mineo might have taken.

It's certainly possible to see that had *The Conqueror* never been made its stars could have gone on to longer careers and greater roles. John Wayne, Susan Hayward, Dick Powell, Agnes Moorehead and Pedro Armendariz all could have lived long and healthy lives giving us more screen classics to remember them by.

Cleopatra might not have left Twentieth Century Fox near bankruptcy in 1963 and the romance and movies of Elizabeth Taylor and Richard Burton might never have taken place. And for Montgomery Clift, the accident that nearly took his life and left him in such pain may never had happened had he not made *Raintree County* with Elizabeth Taylor. And hopefully, lessons have been learned from the effects drugs had on the lives of Marilyn Monroe and Montgomery Clift.

Of course, speculation is meaningless and the fact is, these films will live on for years regardless, giving us images of fantastic entertainers and classic motion pictures with stories that will continue to thrill and fascinate us forever.

Bibliography

Books

Blatty, William Peter. *William Peter Blatty on 'The Exorcist:' From Novel to Film.* 1974. New York, Bantam Books.

Bosworth, Patricia. *Montgomery Clift.* 1978. New York. Bantam Books.

Brodsky, Jack; Weiss, Nathan. *The Cleopatra Papers.* 1963. NewYork. Simon and Schuster.

Brown, Peter Harry; Barham, Patter B. *Marilyn: The Last Take.* 1992. New York. Dutton Books.

Castle, William. *Step Right Up - I'm Gonna Scare the Pants off America.* 1976. New York Pharos Books.

Considine, Shaun. *Bette & Joan: The Divine Feud.* 1989.

New York. Dell Publishing.

Drosnin, Michael. *Citizen Hughes.* 1985. New York. Bantam Books.

Harris, Robert A.; Lasky, Michael S. *The Films of Alfred Hitchcock.* 1976. New York. Citadel Press.

Harris, Warren G. *Natalie & R.J.* 1988. New York. Dolphin Books.

Heymann, C. David. *Liz.* 1995. New York. Birch Lane Press.

Humphries, Patrick. *The Films of Alfred Hitchcock.* 1986. New Jersey. Crescent Books.

Hyams, Joe. *James Dean: Little Lost Boy.* 1992. New York. Warner Books.

Kapsis, Robert E. *Hitchcock: The Making of a Reputation.* 1992. Chicago. The University of Chicago Press.

LaGuardia, Robert. *Monty.* 1977. New York. Avon Books.

Laguardia, Robert. *Red: The Tempestuous Life of Susan Hayward.* 1985. New York. Macmillan Publishing Company.

Madsen, Axel. *John Huston.* 1978. New York. Doubleday & Company.

Martinetti, Ronald *The James Dean Story.* 1975. New York. Pinnacle Books.

Medved, Harry and Michael.*The Hollywood Hall of Shame.* 1984. New York. Perigee Books.

Murray, Eunice. *Marilyn: The Last Months.* 1975. New York. Pyramid Books.

Newquist, Roy. *Conversations With Joan Crawford.* 1980. New York. The Citadel Press.

Petrou, David Michael. *The Making of Superman.* 1978. New York. Warner Books.

Shepherd, Donald; Slatzer, Robert. *Duke: The Life and Times of John Wayne.* 1985. New York. Zebra Books.

Spada, James. *Monroe.* 1982. New York. Dolphin Books.

Spoto, Donald. *The Dark Side of Genius: The Life of Alfred Hitchcock.* 1983. New York. Ballantine Books.

Spoto, Donald. *The Art of Alfred Hitchcock.* 1992. New York. Anchor Books.

Stacy, Pat. *Duke: A Love Story.* 1983. New York. Pocket Books.

Stallings, Penny. *Flesh and Fantasy.* 1978. New York. St. Martin's Press.

Summers, Anthony. *Goddess.* 1985. New York. Macmillan Publishing Company.

Thomas, Bob. *Joan Crawford.* 1978. New York. Bantam Books.

Walker, Alexander. *Elizabeth .* 1990. New York. Grove Weidenfeld.

Wood, Lana. *Natalie.* 1984. G.P. Putnam's Sons.

Magazines, Newspapers and Transcripts

Adler, Renata. "Screen: 'Rosemary's Baby,' a Story of Fantasy and Horror," *The New York Times*. June 13, 1968.

Arnold, Gary. "'Exorcist II': Giving the Devil His Due." *The Washington Post*. June 18, 1977.

Baker, Phil. "'Joan Crawford: The Last Word' Book Review." *Sunday Times*. April 7, 1996

Brisbane, Arthur S. "Violent Dath Plague Old 'Exorcist' Haunts. *The Washington Post*. May 6, 1985.

Cagle, Jess. "Joan Crawford: The 'Mildred Pierce' Actress Saved Her Best Performance for Oscar Night." *Entertainment Weekly*. March, 1996

Canby, Vincent. "Review: 'The Exorcist'." *The New York Times*. December 27, 1973.

Cowan, Geoffrey. "What Do 'Ecstasy' and 'Poltergeist' Have in Common?" *The New York Times*. February 6, 1983.

Churcher, Sharon. "How Did I Do? Asks Superman As He Faces Operation," *Mail on Sunday*. June 4, 1995.

Colburn, Don. "Spinal Cord Injuries. Actor Christopher Reeve's Tragedy Highlights The Devastating Effects." *The Washington Post*. June 6, 1995.

Coppola, Vincent; Friendly, David T.; Huck, Janet. "No, It's Superhype." *Newsweek*. October 9, 1978.

Corrigan, Patricia. "Mime Troupe's Message Sounds Loud and Clear." *St. Louis Post-Dispatch*. May 1, 1989.

Crowther, Bosley. "Last Of A Legend." *The New York Times*. February 5, 1961.

Crowther, Bosley. "Screen: John Huston's 'The Misfits'." *The New York Times*. February 2, 1961.

Curtis, Quentin. "Hitchcock the Romantic: His Films Famously Celebrated and Tortured Women." *The Daily Telegraph*. April 27, 1996.

Davidson, Rose. "Not Fade Away." *Scotland on Sunday*. October 1, 1995.

Deutsch, Linda. "New Book on the Chowchilla Kidnapping." Associated Press. January 18, 1978.

Dougherty, Margot; Podesta, Jane Sims. "That Old Devil William Blatty Is Filming A New Exorcist Like A Man Possessed." *People*. August 14, 1989.

Dressler, Martin. "Tale of an American Dreamer." *The Washington Post*. April 28, 1996.

Drew, Bernard. "John Huston: At 74 No Formulas." *American Film*. September 1980.

Egan, Jack. "Movie Executives Rebut Criticisms of Industry." *The Washington Post*. February 8, 1978.

Esterow, Milton. "R.K.O. Sale Takes A Dramatic Turn," *The New York Times*. January 6, 1956.

Eyman, Scott. "Biography Captures Tragic Life of Lockridge," *The Palm Beach Post*. June 5, 1994.

Fiske, Edward B. "Movie Leads to Requests for Exorcisms." *The New York Times*. January 28, 1974.

Gillins, Peter. "Author Documents Debate Over Government's Utah Atom Tests." *United Press International*. August 5, 1984.

Gold, Sarah. "Doubleday Looks Behind 'The Exorcist'." *Publishers Weekly*. May 3, 1993.

Grover, Stephen. "'Exorcist 2: The Heretic.'" *The Wall Street Journal*. June 30, 1977.

Hughes, Cleora. "Did Ghengis Get Conned in Utah?," *St. Louis Post-Dispatch*. April 20, 1989.

Heymann, David. "She Needed A Man Who Could Dominate. Mike Todd Was The One." *Sun-Sentinel*. April 23, 1995.

Page, Tim. "The Literary Journeys of Father and Son." *Newsday*. November 17, 1994.

Holloron, Jack. "Margot Kidder, 'Insane for Many Years,' Is Back." *News Tribune*. July 29, 1996.

Huard, Christine. "Actress Honored for Efforts to Protect Animals." *The San Diego Union-Times*. June 29, 1995.

Hubbard, Kim; Eftimiades, Maria. "Voyage of Discovery: A Son Explores His Father's Unexplained Suicide." *People*. March 25, 1996.

Hughes, Cleora. "Did Ghengis Get Conned in Utah?," *St. Louis Post-Dispatch*. April 20, 1989.

Indiana, Gary. "Bedeviled," *The Village Voice*. August 29, 1995.

Jennings, Lisa. "Stories About Bunker Hill Road." *United Press International*. May 6, 1985.

Joiner, Lynne. "Star of 'The Birds' Preserves Lives of Wild Animals." *CNN News.* December 26, 1994.

Jones, Welton. " 'Secrets in the Sand' Reveals a Deadly Legacy," *The San Diego Union-Tribune.* April 16, 1989.

Kerh, Dave. "Marnie." *The Chicago Tribune.* October 23, 1986.

Klemesaud, Judy. "Audience Comments on 'The Exorcist' ." *The New York Times.* January 27, 1974.

Kroll, Jack. "Super Star." *Newsweek.* January 1, 1979.

Lee, Shirley. "Tippi Hedren: Nature Girl." *Mature Health.* October, 1989.

Macintyre, Ben. "Reeve's Bones Fused in Spine Surgery." *The Times.* June 6, 1995.

Mal, Vincent. "The Show Must Go On." *The Virginia-Pilot.* May 18, 1994.

Marx, Andy. "Buzz; Lost and Found." *Variety.* August 30, 1993.

McKenna, Kristine. "The Real Death Valley." *Los Angeles Times.* January 19, 1992.

Meeacham, Roy. "Children Barred from 'Exorcist' ." *The New York Times.* February 3, 1974.

Miller, Ron. "A Cool Blond Looks Back." *The Chicago Tribune.* March 20, 1994.

Morris, Gretchen J. "Profiles in Success: Barbara Walden's Ministry of Beauty." *Los Angeles Sentinel.* June 21, 1995.

Moss, Robert T. "Escape from the Zombie Set." *Evening Standard*. April 14, 1984.

Moton, Tony. "She's at Home at the Zoo." *Omaha World Herald*. May 21, 1995.

Musto, Michael. "Grand Dames - Guingo!" *The Village Voice*. September 5, 1995.

Nelson, W. Dale. "Demons, Death and Exorcists Romp Through Georgetown." Associated Press. August 23, 1989.

Nicholls, Liz. "Blair Tries to Exorcise Demons of the Role that Made Her." *The Vancouver Sun*. April 18, 1995.

O'Connor, John J. "TV Weekend." *The New York Times*. March 6, 1981.

Paddock, Richard C. "The Long, Chilling Shadow of Manson." *Los Angeles Times*. August 6, 1994.

Parker, John. "Get Ready, Said Charles Manson, Your're On The Devil's Business." *Daily Mail*. June 25, 1994.

Powers, Thomas. "'Atomic Harvest' Book Review." *The Atlantic*. March 1994.

Romney, Jonathan. "Roman Empire in Exile." *The Guardian*. April 13, 1995.

Rosenblatt, Roger. "Margo Kidder." *The Newshour with Jim Lehrer*. May 6, 1996.

Saltus, Richard. "Prospects Brighter For Paralyzed." *The Plain Dealer*. June 6, 1995.

Silverman, Jeff. "Bad Timing, But Heaven Can Wait." *The Observer*. June 5, 1994.

Simon, Jeff. "Kiss of Death." *The Buffalo News.* December 27, 1995.

Scott, Vernon. "Scott's World Blonde Recalls Hitchcock." U.P.I. March 2, 1985.

Scott, Vernon. "The Exorcist Girl Talks Frankly to *Photoplay*." *Photoplay.* October 1977.

Soltis, Andy. "Brando's Life of Bounty Now a Greek Tragedy." *The Boston Herald.* April 18, 1995.

Sotero, Ray. "Revisiting Bus Kidnapping." Gannett News Service. January 30, 1992.

Spillman, Susan. "'Exorcist III,' a No. 1 Box-Office Force." *USA Today.* August 21, 1990.

Squadrito, Cheryl. "The Death of a Young Star Can Be A Marketing Windfall." *The Record.* August 22, 1994.

Squires, Sally. "Helmets Offer No Protection Against Spinal Cord Injuries." *The Washington Post.* June 6, 1995.

Stack, Peter. "Still A 'Rebel' After All These Years." *San Francisco Chronicle.* May 10, 1995.

Sugarman, Carol. "Style: Personalities." *The Washington Post.* August 7, 1979.

Suplee, Curt. "Reeve Undergoes Surgery to Prevent Further Injury." *The Washington Post.* June 6, 1995.

Thomas, Bob. "Star of Hitchcock Thriller Keeps Blood Stirring In Own Private Jungle." *Los Angeles Times.* July 3, 1994.

Thomas, Bob. "Hollywood." *Associated Press.* August 6,

1979.

Staff Reports. "Magazine Notes High Cancer Rate Among Actors At Utah Site." Associated Press. November 2, 1980.

Thompson, Douglas. "Manson: 'I'm Still Waiting To Kill'." *Sunday Mirror*. July 31, 1994.

Torgerson, Dial. "Sharon Tate, Four Others Murdered." *Los Angeles Times*. August 10, 1969.

Weiler, A. H. "Screen: 'Trog'." *The New York Times*. October 29, 1970.

Wiley, Walt. "Study Shows How James Dean Really Dies." *San Francisco Examiner.* April 23, 1995.

Staff Reports. "Actress Margot Kidder Sues Over Injuries on Set." Associated Press. December 7, 1990.

Staff Reports. "Outlook For '95." *Daily Variety*. January 5, 1995.

Staff. "Filming of 'The Exorcist'." *The New York Times*. August 15, 1972.

Staff. "Friedkin on 'The Exorcist'." *The New York Times*. August 27, 1972.

Staff. "Tourists Follow Steps, Literally, of 'The Exorcist' ." *The New York Times*. October 28, 1982.

Staff. "Demons in the Suburbs?" United Press International. May 7, 1985.

Staff. "Study: Horror Flicks Trigger Delusions." United Press International. August 25, 1995.

Staff. "William Friedkin and 'Jade' ." Radio TV Reports.

February 22, 1996.

Turan, Kenneth. "A Quick Fix: Hurry Up Help for 'The Heretic';" *The Washington Post.* July 1, 1977.

Van Gelder, Lawrence. "Jack MacGowran, Interpreter of Beckett and O'Casey, Dead." *The New York Times.* January 31, 1973.

Wire Services, "Cheyenne Brandon Is A Suicide; Actor's Daughter, 25, Hangs Self in Tahiti." *The Washington Post.* April 18, 1995.

Wire Services, "Margot Kidder Talks Candidly About Breakdown." Reuters. September 13, 1996.

Wire Services, "Midday Headlines," City News Service. April 24, 1996.

Wire Services, "Margot Kidder Recovering in Montana." States News Briefs. July 30, 1996.

Wire Services. "Actor Christopher Reeve to Undergo Surgery." Reuters. June 5, 1995.

Wire Services. "Man Who Kidnapped, Buried Schoolchildren Denied Parole." *The San Diego Union Tribune.* June 8, 1989.

Wire Services. "Chowchilla Kidnapping." Associated Press. December 16, 1977.

Word, Ron. "Similarities Between 'Exorcist II' and Murders Raised." Associated Press. March 17, 1994.

Tragedy and Disaster Behind the Movies

Index

Above Suspicion 124
Adams, Nick 56
Albert, Eddie 118
Aldrich, Robert 115
Anger, Kenneth 17
Apocalypse Now 115
Asner, Ed 118
Armendariz. Pedro 78, 79, 80, 82, 126
Atkins, Susan 15
Atomic Energy Commission 76, 79, 83
Backus, Jim 56
Balsam, Martin 118

Bara, Theda 43
Bardot, Brigitte 44
Barker, Tim 83
Beatty, Ned 116
Beausoleil, Bobby 17
Beck, John 116
Ben-Hur 44
Benton, Robert 115
Bergen, Candice 14
Bergen, Polly 123
Berserk 90, 93
The Birds 34, 35, 37, 38
Birdt, Marvin 8
Blackmer, Sidney 10
Blair, Linda 101-107

Blatty, William Peter 100-108
The Bold and the Beautiful 38
Bonnie and Clyde 115
Boorman, John 107
Bougeau, Francois Robert 109
Boyd, Stephen 44, 45
Brainstorm 60, 61
Brando, Cheyenne 122-123
Brando, Christian 122-123
Brando, Marlon 52, 77, 115-117, 122-123
The Bridge on the River Kwai 72
Bridges, Jeff 116
Brooks, Richard 68
Burstyn, Ellen 101, 103, 106
Burton, Richard 43-50, 106-107, 126
Butterfield 8 45, 47, 71
The Caine Mutiny 68
Camelot 45
Canby, Vincent 12
The Caretakers 89
Castle, William 7-17, 89-90, 125
Cassavettes, John 10, 11
Chapman, Mark David 17
The Chicago Tribune 39
Clark, Caroll 83
Clark, Ricky Peter 109
Clayburg, Jill 116
Cleopatra 43-50, 126
Clift, Montgomery 3, 23, 27, 65-72, 126
Cobb, Lee J. 101, 108
Cohen, Herman 90, 92, 93
Colbert, Claudette 43, 93
Collins, Joan 44
Columbo 60
The Conqueror 2, 75-84, 126
Cooper, Jackie 118
Coppola, Francis Ford 115
Costner, Kevin 2
The Countess From Hong Kong 38
Crawford, Joan 9, 26, 87-95, 126
David, Bud and Mildred 83
Davis, Bette 89
Day, Doris 14
Day, Ellen 108
Dean, James 51-61, 126
Dietrich, Marlene 93
DiMaggio, Joe 22
Dinner at Eight 90
Dmytryk, Edward 68, 71, 72
Donner, Richard 115-121
Doran, Ann 56
Dracula 8
Dream On 38
Drollet, Dag 122
Dunaway, Faye 88
East of Eden 52
Eastwood, Clint 116
Esquire 22
Exodus 59

The Exorcist 3, 99-109, 115, 122, 126
The Exorcist II - The Heretic 106-107
Exorcist: 1990 108
Family Plot 37
Farrow, Mia 11, 16
Finch, Peter 44, 45
Fisher, Carrie 116
Fisher, Eddie 46, 47
Fletcher, Louise 106-107
Folger, Abigale 15
Fonda, Jane 101
Ford, Glenn 94
Frankenstein 92
Freeman, Dore 94
Freidkin, William 101-106, 115
Frenzy 37
From Here to Eternity 22, 72
Frykowski, Voytek 15
Gable, Clark 3, 21-28, 125
Gable, Kay 27
Garretson, William 15
Gerson, Jeanne 82
Giant 58, 59, 72, 106
Ginsberg, Henry 58
The Godfather 115
Gone With The Wind 22, 65, 71
Gordon, Ruth 10
Griffith, Melanie 33, 38
Guillerman, John 115
Guy, Raymond 93
Hackman, Gene 116

Haiami, Shahrokh 14
Hamilton, Guy 115
Hatch, Senator Orrin 83
Hayward, Susan 75-84, 126
Hedren, Tippi 31-39
Hinman, Gary 16, 17
Hitchcock, Alfred 1, 9, 31-39,
Hoffman, Robert 108
Horrors of the Black Museum 90
House on Haunted Hill 8
Hudson, Rock 58, 68
Hughes, Howard 75, 76, 81, 83
Hughes, Reverend Albert 100
Hunter, Tab 56
Huston, John 23-28
I Saw What You Did 8
I Was a Teenage Werewolf 90
I'll Cry Tomorrow 71
The Iron Major 90
Ivanhoe 71
Jailhouse Rock 72
Jaws 115
Jenner, Bruce 116
Jet Pilot 81
JFK 3
Johnny Guitar 52, 106
Kandel, Aben 90
Kaufman, Millard 67
Kasabian, Linda 15
Kelly, Grace 32, 34, 35
Kidder, Margot 113-124
King, Perry 116

Klugman, Jack 118
Knife in the Water 9
The Knute Rockne Story 90
Komeda, Christopher 13
Krenwikle, Patricia 15
Kristopherson, Kris 116
Kubrick, Stanley 101
LaBianca, Leno and Rosemary 16, 17
Lange, Jessica 116
Legion 107
Leigh, Janet 32, 39
Leigh, Vivien 66
Lennon, John 17
Let's Make Love 23
Levin, Ira 7
Lindner, Robert 52
Lockridge, Ross 66 - 67
Lollobrigida, Gina 44
Lucifer Rising 17
Lugosi, Bela 8
MacLaine, Shirley 101, 116
Mame 82
Mamoulian, Rouben 45
Mankiewicz, Joseph 45
Mansfield, Jayne 56
Manson, Charles 2, 14, 15, 125
Mary Rose 36, 37
Matthau, Walter 118
Mazzola, Frank 59
MCA 33
McCaimbridge, Mercades 106
McCarthy, Kevin 68-69

McClure, Mark 116
McGowran, Jack 102-104
McKenna, Ken 67
McQueen, Steve 116
Melcher, Terry 14, 15
MGM 35, 45, 65, 67, 68, 70, 72, 87, 88
Mildred Pierce 88-89
Miles, Vera 32
Miller, Arthur 22, 23, 24, 126
Miller, Jason 101
Minelli, Liza 116
Mineo, Sal 51, 56, 58-60, 126
The Misfits 21-28, 125
Mommie Dearest 88, 89
Monroe, Marilyn 3, 21-28, 44, 125, 126
Money Train 3
Montand, Yves 23
Moorehead, Agnes 78, 80, 82, 126
Nelson, Lori 56
The New York Times 12, 94
Newman, David and Leslie 115
Newman, Paul 116
Newquist, Roy 26, 89
Nichols, Mike 101
Nicholson, Jack 10
Nixon 3
Nolte, Nick 116
North By Northwest 32, 71
Novak, Kim 32, 39
Olive Medical Center 123

O'Neal, Ryan 116
The Out of Towners 13
Pacific Heights 38
Paramount Studios 9, 10, 11, 12
Pendleton, Dr. Robert 80
Penn, Arthur 101
Pepsi Cola 90, 92
Perrine, Valerie 116
Photoplay 36
Pinewood Studios 118
A Place in the Sun 66
Planer, John 109
The Plough and the Stars 103
Polanski, Roman 7-17, 125
Powell, Dick 78, 80, 82, 126
Price, Vincent 9
P.S. Your Cat is Dead 60
Psycho 1, 9, 32, 33, 34
Puzo, Mario 115
Raines, Christina 116
Raintree County 3, 65-72, 126
Ray, Nicholas 52, 55-57
Rear Window 22
Rebel Without A Cause 2, 51-61, 126
Redford, Robert 10, 116
Reeve, Christopher 113-124
Reynolds, Burt 116
Reynolds, Debbie 47, 56, 82
Ritter, Thelma 23, 24
RKO 77, 78, 81
Roar 38
Robards, Jason 118

Rosemary's Baby 3, 7-17, 125
Saint, Eva Marie 32
Salkind, Alexander and Ilya 114
Schary, Dore 67
Schoenfeld, James and Richard 105
Scott, George C. 108
Sebring, Jay 15
The Seven Year Itch 22
Shea, Donald 16
Shelton, Darrenna 109
Shepperton Studios 116
Shulman, Irving 55
Simon, Neil 13
Sinatra, Frank 10, 11, 16
Skouras, Spyros 44, 49
Smith, Dick 104
Soul, David 116
The Sound of Music 50
Spengler, Pierre 114
Spielberg, Steven 115
Stanwyck, Barbara 9
Star Wars 116
Steele, Alfred 92
Stone, Oliver 3
Strait-Jacket 8, 89
Streisand, Barbra 116
Suddenly Last Summer 66
Superman 3, 94, 113-124, 126
Superman II 118-121
Superman III 122
Superman IV 122
Tate, Sharon 14, 15, 16, 17, 125

Taylor, Elizabeth 3, 43-50, 58, 65-72, 126
That's Entertainment 87
13 Ghosts 8
The Three Musketeers 114, 119
Through the Eyes of a Killer 38
The Tingler 8
Today 33
Todd, Mike 46, 70
Topaz 37
Torn Curtain, 37
The Towering Inferno 115
Trog 87-95, 126
Truffaut, Francois 37
Twelve Angy Men 72
Twentieth Century Fox 43, 77, 126
Uris, Leon 55
Variety 105
Velasquez, Danny 109
Vertigo 32
von Sydow, Max 101
Wagner, Robert 60, 116
Walken, Christopher 60
Wallach, Eli 23, 24
Warbeck, David 91
Warner Bros. 51, 52, 55, 56, 57, 58, 89, 105, 106, 122
Warner Communications 114-115
Warren, Leslie Ann 116
Washington Post 99
Waterworld 2

Watson, Tex 15
Wayne, John 75-84, 126
Wayne, Michael 83
Wayne, Patrick 83
Weakley, Della 109
Weld, Tuesday 10
What Ever Happened to Baby Jane? 89, 115
White, Christine 56
Who Killed Teddy Bear? 60
Wicked Stepmother 87
Wilding, Michael 68, 70
Williams, Lionel R. 66
Wilson, Dennis 14
Wood, Lana 56
Wood, Natalie 51, 56, 60-61, 116, 126
Woodcock, Scott 109
Woods, Fred 105
Woodward, Joanne 44
The Wrong Man 32
Wyler, William 68
Wynn, Keenan 118
York, Susanna 116
Zanuck, Darryl 49

Tragedy and Disaster Behind the Movies

About the Author

John Law is an editor and journalist whose work has appeared in newspapers, magazines and books. In all, he has worked on the staffs of six daily, three weekly and several monthly publications. He has also been the editor of several books. As a freelance writer his work has appeared in various magazines and newspapers. He frequently writes on the film and entertainment industry and is currently working on a book on the life and films of director William Castle.

MOVIE GIVEAWAY CONTEST

Enter the *Curse of the Silver Screen* Movie Giveaway Contest by sending your name, address and daytime phone number to:

Curse of the Silver Screen Movie Giveaway Contest
P.O. Box 210126
San Francisco, CA 94121

Winners will be selected at random throughout the sale of the *Curse of the Silver Screen — Tragedy & Disaster Behind the Movies.* Winners will receive video copies of films chronicled in the book, such as *The Exorcist, Rosemary's Baby, TheConqueror* and more.